TAFOLLA TORO

TAFOLLA TORO

TORO

THREE YEARS
OF FEAR

LORENZO GOMEZ, III

TAFOLLA TORO

Three Years of Fear

ISBN   978-1-5445-0516-9 *Hardcover*

      978-1-5445-0517-6 *Paperback*

      978-1-5445-0515-2 *Ebook*

This book is dedicated to Doug Robins and Marney DeFoore.

Thank you for being my guides on the road to recovery.

CONTENTS

INTRODUCTION

THE END OF INNOCENCE

It's 1992. I'm eleven years old, and Mari is nine years old. I'm listening to Blind Melon's new song No Rain.

When I was in fifth grade, my younger sister, Mari, and I would walk home from Woodrow Wilson Elementary School together. The elementary school day let out before the middle and high schools, so we normally didn't see other students on our way home. We had to walk across the Interstate 10 bridge to reach our house, which was on West Hermosa—which ironically means beautiful in Spanish—but there was nothing beautiful about my dead-end street in San Antonio, Texas. We would always hold hands as we crossed the bridge and it was my daily reminder that I was her big brother. And a good big brother always protects his little sister.

On this day, from the moment the school bell rang, we knew something was wrong. Mari and I had walked home across that bridge more than a hundred times. It was always empty, and all we could hear were the cars passing below. On this day, we saw something we had never seen before, a crowd of big kids—that's what we called the middle and high school students—and they were everywhere. As we approached the bridge, the big kids came up behind us as if they had decided to walk home with us that day. There must have been fifty guys around, ahead of, and behind us. Mari squeezed my hand and whispered, "Lencho, why are all these big kids out?" All I could say was, "I don't know." As we walked up the bridge, we saw another fifty big kids coming from the other side of the bridge.

I kept my head down and gripped Mari's hand tighter. We moved to the edge to avoid getting swept up in the crowd. We were surrounded by the big kids, and they didn't notice us. I felt like we were two ghosts passing in between them. Like they could have walked right through us if they had wanted. That is, if they had even noticed us. As we scurried home, all I could see were Red Wing cowboy boots, the $200 boots construction workers buy once every ten years. I don't really know why I remember that detail. I think I was so afraid, that I didn't want to look the big kids in the eye. Because I was staring down, all I could see were their shoes.

We got to our front door. If an adult had been home, we would have been told to go inside. I knew we should have, but our curiosity was too strong. Mari and I stood on the step, still wearing our backpacks that were bigger than we were, and watched. We saw them gather and realized it was two massive groups of kids coming toward each other, and then they stopped. It was so insane, I wondered if they were filming a movie, but I quickly realized this was real. They all stood there still and quiet, while it looked like a couple of them talked to each other. Then, as if lightning had struck, an explosion of fists, yelling, rushing. The bridge, which had chain-link fence covering the top and both sides, became the scene for a hundred-man cage fight.

Almost as soon as it started, a half dozen cop cars pulled up on each end of the bridge, closing off any direct escape. The big kids then started to do things I didn't think were humanly possible. They jumped off the top of the bridge like comic book superheroes, onto the access road below. They ran and leaped over six-foot fences to get away from the cops. The cops could only catch a fraction of these guys. As I watched I thought, "Wow, that's the power of Red Wing boots. If I had Red Wing boots, I could do everything those guys did. I could be tough." Later, my friend told me that it had been a fight between two gangs: the LenchMob and the Kings.

Before I saw that fight, school had been about learning—I

thought the only thing I had to worry about was being a good student and being well behaved. The fight on the bridge was the flicker of something I didn't understand about my environment-to-come that would leave me terrified. I thought for sure that this fight had to be a once in a lifetime thing. As I prepared for middle school I hoped and prayed that I would never see anything that big and uncontrollable ever again.

THE HARVARD OF MIDDLE SCHOOLS

I was supposed to go to Whittier Middle School because it was closest to my house. In the San Antonio Independent School District (SAISD) world, that made it my "home school." But my parents knew from experience that it wasn't exactly the best school in the district. My older sister Denise had gone to Whittier. One night at dinner, Denise proudly told my family that she helped a classmate roll cigarettes just like she'd done for Grandpa Gomez in Laredo. When my brothers burst her bubble and explained that she was unknowingly rolling joints, my parents decided none of their other children would go to Whittier. It was a shame, too, because the guy told Denise that hers were the tightest, best-rolled joints he had ever had.

My parents had plans for me to go to college, so when my mom said, "There's this new, multilingual program in Tafolla Middle School," I was excited even though I'd never heard of any of those words. I didn't know what Tafolla was, and I didn't know what a multilingual program was. Mom explained, "You can learn a foreign language." I immediately thought, "This is special. I can finally learn Spanish."

A lot of Hispanics of my generation didn't learn to speak Spanish as children. The San Antonio school district had an informal policy saying they would only admit students who spoke English. So, many Spanish-speaking parents stopped teaching their children Spanish. A whole generation of Hispanic children grew up without this piece of their culture. My own family felt this first hand. There are seven kids in my family and the first three, Danny, Denise, and Mark, all spoke Spanish as their first language. But when my mother put them in school, she was told that if they didn't speak English, the school would not accept them. So the rest of us all were taught English only. I've often felt that I am a broken Mexican, because I don't speak my mother tongue. As I filled out my application for Tafolla, I said, "I want to speak Spanish." I desperately wanted to fit in. Mom was thinking about college and said, "No, you're going to learn Latin because Latin will help you break down words forever. It'll help you on your SATs and in whatever you decide to study in college." I fought her, but in the end, she was the boss. My Grandma Petra, who had the best sense of humor, teased my mom, "Who's he going to speak Latin to? The Pope?"

When I applied and got in, it was one of the highlights of my young life. To me, going to this multilingual program sounded like getting accepted into college, and I later learned the principal proudly called Tafolla the "Harvard of Middle Schools."

I was happy about going to Tafolla, but I was also nervous. I wondered, "Will I live up to the specialness of this school? Am I really that smart? I know my fifth-grade teacher thinks I'm that smart, but will there be other teachers like her there? I don't know." I was excited, but the anticipation made me more nervous.

SHE WANTED ME TO BE BRAVE

Being nervous about going to school wasn't new for me. I'd been nervous the night before going to kindergarten. I remember Mom helping me put my things together for the next day. She remembered the first day of school for all of her seven children. The one that stood out most was my older brother Mark's first day of school. She was trying to encourage me when she said how brave he was. She said Mark wouldn't let her go in with him, and he said, "No, no, Mom, I'm okay. Go home. I got this," and he just marched in the school. The rest of the Gomez clan, on the other hand, were crying, soggy messes on our first day of school.

I remember thinking, "She wants me to be like Mark. She wants me to be brave." I didn't feel brave. I was scared, and I was nervous, but I put on a brave face for my first day of kindergarten. At five years old, I already was pretending to be someone I wasn't.

As an adult, I now know I was telling myself a lie. I should have said, "Mom, I'm really nervous and scared," and let her say, "It's okay for you to be nervous and scared." The fact that I didn't speak up was the start of some bad habits in my thinking. My desire to not worry my mom was greater than the fear I was feeling. I unconsciously created a false story in my head, which was, "This is what she wants me to do, and I need to be this other person that I'm not."

I carried that fear and anxiety with me. I loved fifth grade, but I was very nervous and scared about middle school. I didn't weigh more than a hundred pounds until after I graduated high school. After seeing the fight on the bridge, I was even more aware of how small and weak I was. If being brave meant being in a fight like the one the bridge, then I was in big trouble. I should probably get some Red Wing boots pronto.

REMEMBERING MY PAST

Noted author and pastor Dr. Timothy Keller says that there are certain thoughts in your head that are like carbon monoxide; they're odorless and tasteless and before you know it, they've poisoned your mind. That's what happened to me. In middle school, my nervousness and anxiety tipped. I had all kinds of thoughts in my head about who I was supposed to be and who the people around me were—many of them exaggerated, most of them untrue—that poisoned me in the years to come. The more I told myself stories about the things that were going on, the worse it got.

I was so afraid and had so much anxiety during those three years of middle school that I completely blocked out my memories of that time. I simply refused to remember those years. As an adult, I decided to go to therapy to work on the unhealthy behaviors I had developed in my life. I thought I had a problem with anger, addiction, and depression, but through therapy I realized those were symptoms. There was a deeper cause underneath those symptoms, and that was my paralyzing fear.

I started thinking about that three-year period of middle school that I'd completely wiped out. I began to remember the extreme fear and anxiety I had in my early years of adolescence, from age twelve to fifteen, and I saw how those three years that I'd completely forgotten had a huge impact on the man I'd become.

When I went into therapy, one of the first things my therapist asked me to do was write down the narrative of my life, beginning with my earliest memories about things like when I started school, who took me, and how I felt. When I started writing about my first day of school, I realized it was the answer to everything that was to come.

This is the story of the years I forgot, and how I made sense of them. Everything I went through then shaped everything that came after.

YOUR STORY

Adults tend to underestimate young people in general. I want you to know that I see the adult in you no matter what your age is. If you picked up this book, I believe you're ready to think about the stories I tell and how they might help you see your own story. You might be feeling things but don't have the language you need to talk about it. You might be angry, or you might be scared.

You might be nodding your head because you recognize yourself in my story, or maybe you're too cool for school and think this is just part of growing up. Either way, I know a part of you is listening and I want to tell you this: A journey to mental health can start at any age. A healthy body is useless without a healthy mind. That is what this book is about. Think about your own story and the story you tell yourself as you read mine.

PS: At the end of each chapter, the adult Lorenzo that I am today has written a letter to my younger self, Lench or Lencho. I want to give him—and you—some insight about what was really going on as opposed to what young Lorenzo believed was happening at the time. If you only had room to stuff a couple of pages in your backpack, the letters are the ones I'd want you to take with you and go back to when you're struggling.

CHAPTER 1

~~~~~~~

FIRST DAY OF MIDDLE SCHOOL

It's 1993, and I'm twelve years old. The song in my head-phones is Today *by The Smashing Pumpkins.*

I had a sickening, panicked idea that middle school would be completely unfamiliar, but the multilingual program was also supposed to be a great opportunity, so I had hopes that it would be exciting and fun. The bus ride sobered me up real quick. Before I even reached the school itself, I found myself already fighting to keep my hopes high with excitement.

The first day, I went to Whittier Middle School like a normal student and then boarded the Route Five bus to Tafolla Middle School. A couple people I knew, including my friends Joe and Daniel, were also on the bus, so at least I had a couple friends. I immediately noticed that I had to learn some new behaviors. It was like prison yard rules, but for the bus. Everyone had their distinct territory: sixth graders here, bus driver there, and so forth. The sixth graders sat in the front, the seventh graders sat in the middle, and I shouldn't even think about going to the back of the bus until I became an eighth-grader. The bus driver had rules too. If you wanted to talk to the bus driver, you had to sit down behind the yellow line.

Over the next three years, I all but memorized that bus route, but on that first day, it was like taking a bus to a different country. We took off from Whittier and turned left on Fredericksburg Road. I only remember that because that was the corner where HEB #5 was, the grocery store where my brother Danny had worked. There was a long stretch of the trip on Zarzamora Street, and as we drove down, I took it all in. Watching the streets go by reminded me of the song *Under the Bridge* by The Red Hot Chili Peppers. The first part of Zarzamora had lots and lots of *fruterias*. It made me feel good because what's not to love about chili covered fruit and corn with mayo? The next big milestone was the Basilica of the National Shrine of the Little Flower, but there was nothing little about it. This was the first time I had ever seen anything historic, and this Catholic church looked like our version of the castle from the Walt Disney movies. It was the most beautiful building I had ever seen in the whole world. As we got closer to Tafolla, the type of stores changed. They went from brightly colored *fruterias* to payday loans and tire repair shops. The tire shops were all yellow or blue in color with big names like Trevino Tire Repair. Every shop displayed brand new rims outside the shop, and I thought to myself, "Aren't they worried someone is going to steal those rims?" They looked more expensive than the entire building. But what did I know? I was just a kid.

I thought my own neighborhood was rough, but as we got closer to Tafolla, I felt like the neighborhoods were getting worse. One of the oldest government housing projects in the country—which Eleanor Roosevelt had helped to establish in 1939—stood across the street from the school. Its name was the Alazán-Apache Courts, which I thought sounded like Alcatraz, the prison. These courts also happened to sit in the poorest ZIP code of San Antonio. I heard the Peace Corps used to send people to this area before sending them abroad, to simulate third-world conditions.

From every classroom window that faced north, you could see the tallest building in all of the Westside of San Antonio: the Bexar County Adult Detention Center, otherwise known as the county jail. I did not like seeing the jail every day. It was as if the jail was proclaiming to all the students: you will either run from me or graduate to me.

I stared out the window as the bus pulled up to Tafolla. I stayed in my seat when the door whooshed open, and waited for the other kids to get off the bus. When the last kid passed my seat, I grabbed my backpack and pulled up the end of the line. Despite the neighborhood, the clean brick front of Tafolla looked like a well-kept university, and as with all public buildings, the US flag waved proudly from the pole.

A crowd of kids, mostly bigger than me, stumbled down the sidewalk toward the front doors of the school. I'd seen a documentary on TV about cattle being herded and pushed onto a truck. I felt like those cows probably felt. Some kids yelled to friends from the previous year. I pulled my class schedule out of my back pocket to double-check my homeroom number even though I'd memorized it two weeks earlier.

I was pulled along by the crowd toward a main hallway. The inside of the school matched the well-kept exterior. It smelled like cleaning products. The floors looked like they'd been waxed in preparation for the start of a new school year.

I found my homeroom and the knot in my stomach started to rise to my throat. I looked around the room for a familiar face and quickly realized that out of my small group of friends from Whittier Middle School, I

word to me, even though one sat in the chair to my right and another to my left. They carried on their conversation as if I didn't exist. Did they not see me? It was the exact ghost-like feeling I had on the bridge. I tried to look at them without making eye contact, tried to figure out what my next move should be, how quickly I could get out if things got rough. I didn't know how to act, so I tried to stay as cool and invisible as I could. I thought that maybe if I held my breath, they wouldn't see me.

Their leader sat down directly across from me. He must have flunked a grade more than once. These guys were all Hispanic, but this guy, whom they called José, was *really* Hispanic. He had a goatee—what fourteen-year-old has a goatee? His black hair was slicked back into a short ponytail. His flannel shirt was open at the collar and showed the white T-shirt underneath. I couldn't help but stare, because I was fascinated with this man, the very definition of a *cholo* gangster, masquerading as an eighth-grader.

At the same time, I was alarmed. José stared at me in silence. I had seen that look before but only on TV. It's the look a cheetah gets when it's about to chase a gazelle. Its eyes lock on and nothing can distract its eyes from the prey. His black eyes shimmered, and he had a slightly crooked mouth that could mean he was getting ready to smile or plotting how to torture you.

As I watched Jose and his band of merry men clown around, I had a big realization that no one had told me and that I wasn't prepared for. José and his friends were from the neighborhood, from the Alazán-Apache Courts across the street.

Two distinct populations of students attended Tafolla: the multilingual students like me who were bussed in from different middle schools throughout the SAISD, and then the kids from the neighborhood, whom over time we referred to as the "regulars."

San Antonio was in the midst of a ten-year period of gang violence. I was familiar with gangs. I'd seen that fight go down on the bridge just a few months before. As I watched José's crew, I was trying to figure out if these guys were more dangerous than the ones I was used to or less dangerous, and right away I thought they were more dangerous.

One by one, his posse went silent. One of his friends sitting to my left said, "Hey José, how come you're not eating, bro?" José looked at me like I was a stray dog covered in fleas, and then he said, "I don't like eating in front of people I don't know." Everyone turned and looked at me as if they hadn't noticed me until that very moment.

I had no idea what to do, but I knew I wasn't welcome. I

looked around, then slowly stood up and left the table. I dumped my tray in the trash and walked out. I found a bench in the courtyard right next to a door into the school. I sat down, put on my headphones, and listened to the song *Hunger Strike* by Temple of the Dog. I never ate lunch at school again until I was a senior in high school.

ONE TIME ONLY

Sometime toward the end of the day, I went to the bathroom. I was scared I'd meet another unwelcoming gang, but I had to go, so I went.

The clean appearance of Tafolla ended at the bathroom door. What I saw in the bathroom was what I would guess—not having seen them—the bathrooms were like in Bexar County Jail. There were puddles of urine on the floor. Most of the stalls didn't have doors. I saw only one roll of toilet paper, and it was chained to the stall wall. It was dark and disgusting.

None of the urinals were occupied, but there was no way in hell I was going to pee with my back exposed. I wanted a safe place, so I chose a stall with a door and—to this day I don't know why, maybe I didn't want my back to the door—I sat down to pee. Almost immediately, the door got kicked in and a kid pointed at me and started laughing. Another guy poked his head in and started laughing too. I didn't understand the joke, but I knew they were making fun of me. I didn't feel like they were going to beat me up, but I felt humiliated to be the butt of their joke while I sat there with my pants down. I walked out and immediately added going to the bathroom to my list of things never to do again at school.

T–A–F–O–L–L–A

By the time I got to PE class that day, I was pretty sure the locker room was not going to be a safe place. I did my best to remain invisible. I looked around without looking at anyone. I wanted to change into my gym clothes, stash my backpack, and get out of there as quickly as possible. I went to a section where only one other boy was changing.

At the time, I measured everybody up with the thought, "If I have to fight this person, what are my chances?" This guy was short with a fair build. I wouldn't be able to take him, but he didn't seem like a troublemaker. He wasn't. He was, however, the opposite of a loud-mouthed gangster who wanted to prove himself: he was real danger. He said, "Hey man, I'm Raymond." I said, "I'm Lorenzo," thinking for a moment that I had a chance of making a new friend. Without skipping a beat, he said, "I'm part of the junior Mexican Mafia." I had no idea how to respond to this statement, and it was the very last thing I would have ever guessed to hear on my first day of middle school. He could tell from my shocked blank stare. I didn't want to say the wrong thing, so he broke the silence and said, "Check this out." He opened his backpack so I could look inside. Inside his backpack was the very first handgun I had ever seen up close. Now that I had some more information, I could do some quick street math and break down the situation: Raymond was a sixth-grader from the Alazán-Apache Courts, and he wasn't a multilingual student. He wasn't threatening me, but he clearly wanted to send a message. He wanted me to know that he was in a category of badass that was completely different than everyone else. It was his way of saying, "I'm the most serious guy here and don't forget that." I knew enough to know he wasn't going to have a problem with me as long as I showed him that I wasn't a threat and let him be the alpha.

To that point in the day, I'd been gathering the variables and building a street smart math equation about how to stay safe. Until that moment, I had forgotten that gun violence was a possible variable. I began mapping the known dangers in my brain: multiple people, the neighborhood, and trash talking. Now, there's the danger of being shot with a gun. It was a rookie mistake, and I should have thought of it sooner. Better late than never, I guess.

We changed and went out to the track. The coach started

with jumping jacks and made us spell Tafolla while we jumped.

T
A
F
O
L
L
A,

Tafolla! Tafolla!

After we'd warmed up and memorized how to spell Tafolla, the coach said, "You're going to run three laps around the football field. Go." Growing up, I thought I was pretty good at running but didn't realize how fast I actually was. We took off, and right from the beginning I was smoking everyone; for about a third of the way around the football field, I was the fastest runner. For the first time that day, I was loving life.

Then, in the middle of the second lap, I heard the panting of a runner coming up behind me. As I looked over my shoulder the world went into slow motion, and I saw this kid breeze by me. It was Raymond. He ran without any effort, his feet kicking as high as his lower back. I stared at his back as the distance between us grew. He's the fastest runner in sixth grade, and I was a distant second. I realized not only was he the most dangerous guy here, he was also the most physically superior. A terrifying thought crossed my mind: if for some reason I had a throw down with Raymond, I wouldn't just lose in a fight—I couldn't even *outrun* him.

The saddest part of my first day of school was that I didn't know what to do or not do, because trouble seemed to be looking for me even as I tried to hide from it. The logic that if you minded your own business nothing would happen to you did not seem to work at Tafolla. Suddenly I understood what was going on, like a blind man given sight by Jesus. Tafolla was this special school. But it was also one big obstacle course filled with booby traps. If I wanted to get to the other side, find that specialness, and actually learn something, I was going to have to decide that learning was worth it. I decided to run the gauntlet.

Welcome to the Harvard of Middle Schools.

TORO POWER

One of the few things I loved about Tafolla was the mascot, the Tafolla *Toro*—yes, the book is named after the mascot.

Toro is the Spanish word for bull. The school colors were

red, white, and black, and the Tafolla *Toro* was red and tough-looking, like he was red-hot angry and ready for a fight. I felt a little tougher when I told myself that I, too, was a *toro* like our mascot. A picture of a thing called "The Running of the Bulls" that happens in a town in Spain every year hung on the wall of the social studies classroom. The picture looked dangerous and exciting, and I thought that one day I wanted to run with them too. One day the social studies teacher saw me staring at the picture and told me that Hemingway had a book about it. Maybe one day I will read it.

I loved the mascot not only because I felt tough when I thought of myself as a *Toro* but also because both Mom and Pops have family stories about *toros*, and I loved it when they told them to me.

One of my father's uncles owned a bull named Tiburcio, who was huge, like most bulls, I guess. One day Pops' uncle got a call that Tiburcio had wandered over to a neighboring ranch. He had walked straight through about three different fences. Pops said that once a *toro* puts his head down, nothing can stop him. His uncle walked over to the ranch and the owner looked at him surprised, and said,

"Did you bring a truck and trailer?"

"No," said Pops' uncle.

"Did you bring a rope to lasso him?"

"No."

"How are you going to get him home?"

Pops' uncle pulled out a bowl filled with feed and shook it. As soon as he heard it, Tiburcio walked straight up to Pops' uncle. His uncle walked all the way back to his ranch shaking the bowl of food, and Tiburcio followed him all the way. No rope, no truck.

My mom's story was more dramatic. When she was a little girl, mom's family were all migrant workers. One of the places they worked was a beet farm in North Dakota. Saturday was their day off, so my grandfather Eufracio Jaime, who was very proud that he had all the vowels in his name, gave them three options for pleasure:

They could go to the city dump and look for comic books, dolls, and toys while Grandma Petra looked for dishes. They could go to the movie theater and pay a nickel for "Take a Chance," gambling on the movie that was playing. Or, they could watch Grandpa Eufracio fight the farm's bull.

Mom said Grandpa would use my Tia Delia's red dress as the cape to taunt the bull, and the entire family sat on the corral and cheered for him. He would look at the bull, wave my tia's red dress, and say to him, "*Toro! Se te murió tu mama*," which means, "Bull, your mother is dead."

Every time the bull would make a pass, he made the family yell, "OLE!" and "BRAVO!" Just like I imagine happening at The Running of the Bulls in Spain.

Toro is in my blood: On the Gomez side, we were the tamers of bulls, and on the Jaime side, we were fighters of bulls. I was born to be a Tafolla *Toro*.

On my first day of school, however, I was learning quickly that being a *Toro* was dangerous business. I just hoped I wouldn't let the family down.

ENVIRONMENT, FEAR, AND EXPLORING THE WORLD

DEAR LENCH,

I want to talk about your first day of school. I never realized until a few years ago how very important that first day of school was. The events of that day ended up rewiring your brain for many years to come. Thankfully there is good news. The good news is we can fix any wires that got crossed that day. Let me explain.

Environments can be scary. You stepped on the bus with

the best intentions of going to school, getting an education, and being a part of a special program. Instead, you were faced with a situation and people that no one could have prepared you for. You went into Tafolla thinking it was the Harvard of Middle Schools, but in reality, it felt more like Maximum-Security Middle School.

Let's start with this important truth. That most of the time in life, you don't get to pick a lot of things. You don't get to pick who your parents are. You don't get to pick where you grow up. You don't get to pick how much money or influence your family has or doesn't have. You don't get to pick who your neighbors are. You don't get to pick many things.

On your first day of school, you didn't get to pick the neighborhood your school was in. You didn't get to pick who rode the Route Five bus with you, or who had classes with you. These were all things that the universe conspired to put together, and you had no control over any of it. So, if you think anything that happened on that first day is your fault, I'm here to tell you that it's not true. Let that sink in.

You don't get to pick your environment as a sixth-grader. The only thing you get to pick is how you react to that environment. The only thing that you're in control of is you. There are many things that may make you think you don't have any choices, like the rules and restrictions that parents and schools make us follow. That is not what I am talking about. You're in charge of your emotions and how you express them. But most importantly, you are in charge of the story you tell yourself. It's the difference between saying, "I won't survive at that school," or "The first day was rough but that is in the past. Tomorrow I have decided to give it a new shot." No one can force a story in your head that you do not first allow. It's one of the few things that you don't realize you have total control and autonomy over, which I want you to know absolutely gives you control.

FEAR OF THE UNKNOWN

A Navy SEAL once told a buddy of mine that the greatest fear of all is the fear of the unknown. When people are in that mode, when they don't know something, they become afraid of it.

On your first day, I want to tell you that it was okay to be afraid. You didn't know who was going to be in your classrooms. You didn't know where they were from. You didn't know what their intentions were. You didn't know any of these things, and so, if you were afraid of any of them, that's okay. Because it's human nature to be afraid of the unknown. That's a natural, healthy response.

There is a part of your brain that has been assigned the

job of looking out for fear, and that's why being afraid of the unknown is actually natural and healthy. If you think, "What's wrong with me? I must be defective because I have so much fear." That is not true. That means your body's working.

I am telling you that it was okay for you to be afraid.

Now, I also want to tell you this. If you *stay* afraid, that's the problem.

You probably should have come home and cried, and you didn't, because you probably remembered the story about Mark. You thought you had to be brave.

Ernest Hemingway once said, "A really brave fighting bull is afraid of nothing on earth..." Well guess what, we are not bulls. We are men with complex emotions. And for us, the bravest thing we can do is learn how to process our emotions.

We know that your first day left you feeling scared. I want to tell you that it's okay for you to say that you were terrified. You probably should have gone home that day and told Mom and Pops that it was the worst day ever. But you didn't, and that's okay because it's in the past now. You know what you probably should have done, too? You probably should have cried. You probably should have let it out. We don't know, a lot of times, how to process grief. If you'd have gotten home and broke down and cried, I'm here to tell you that would have been okay, too. Finally, let me tell you what's also okay. It is totally fine that you didn't do any of those things. Why is it fine? Because those things are now in the past and the past has no control over what we do right now. What you decide to do today is all that matters.

YOU STARTED AN ADVENTURE

Let me tell you something else that nobody told you before you started sixth grade: you are on an adventure. When you're on an adventure, nothing is truly safe and that makes them exciting. An adventure has danger, it has highs and lows. You were on an adventure called middle school.

You should have been ready to explore the world, yet when you tried to explore this new world, it turned around and it bit you. It frightened you.

On your first day, we just need to say out loud that you wanted to explore the world, but you felt like it was not safe to explore that world. It's okay that you felt unsafe, but it wasn't a good thing.

In life, you have to be able to explore the world. You can

never lose that part of being a child exploring the world, because that's where learning happens and where relationships form.

I want to tell you that you need to dare to be an adventurer again. The truth is that your first day was scary, but here's what's also true: You survived your first day. You survived it, and no one laid a finger on you. You got back on the bus. You went home. Mom and Pops were there, your brothers and sisters were there. When you walked in the door, you knew they loved you.

Don't forget the good just because some bad things happen to you. Life is still an adventure. You need to remember what's also true in your life. The first day was terrible and traumatizing. There were also a lot of amazing, true things: you had love, respect, and safety at home. You had friends at school; they just weren't with you. There were teachers and administrators and police officers doing things to help you and your classmates, but you hadn't met them yet. They wanted to make the place safe. That's also true.

Remember what's true, and remember that you're on an adventure, and that you will always be on one.

CHAPTER 2

~~~~~

THE LANGUAGE OF
THE STREETS

The moment I walked into Tafolla, I was assigned to an informal gang: the multilingual gang. The local students were part of the informal regulars gang. None of us knew this, of course, but it was the world we walked into. The implication was that if you were a multilingual kid, you were smarter than a regular. Anybody who was already there and knew I was a multilingual student would put me in that group. The regulars weren't saying, "There's Lorenzo, one of those nice, multilingual kids. I should go and be his friend." Instead, they were thinking, "He's one of those guys who's supposed to be smarter than me."

The differences showed up in many ways. The multilingual kids were bussed to school. The local kids mostly *walked* to school. Most of the regulars, if they lived in the Alazán-Apache courts, came from low-income families and were on food stamps, yet many of them wore Red Wing boots, Guess jeans, and Polo shirts. To this day, I don't know how someone on food stamps buys a $200 pair of boots.

A lot of the regulars spoke Spanish, while many of the multilingual kids did not. The regulars knew the language of the streets, and I was about to get a crash course.

I had this notion in my head that the regulars had no boundaries and no structure in their lives. I painted them all with the same brush. I knew I had rules to follow, and these kids did not. I felt like they lived as if the rules didn't apply to them. Whereas I was obsessed with the rules, mostly because I didn't want my parents to get mad at me. Most of the multilingual kids came from middle-class families, and I assumed that they had structure. The regulars seemed to have a different home life—a home life where grandmothers raising kids was more common-place than I was used to seeing.

WHO YOU CLAIMING?

From 1984 to 1997, San Antonio experienced the highest rate of gang violence in its history. The gangs had their territories on the street and that had seeped into the schools. Older brothers brought siblings into the gangs at a young age, and gang members immediately found their safety when they entered a school like Tafolla. If someone asked you the question, "Who do you claim?" they were asking what gang you belonged to.

There were three main gangs that somehow found a way to coexist at Tafolla. The NDs (which might have stood for Notre Dame, but who knows) was the biggest gang in number and in size. Those guys were big, they had muscles, and facial hair. They were everything you shouldn't be in middle school (probably because most of them had repeated a grade or two). While their presence was known at school, they didn't go out of their way to pick fights. They weren't obnoxious, but they were terrifying. They were big, quiet, scary dudes, and they hung out together. They were at the top of the food chain and most of their activity happened on the streets.

Raymond, the guy I met the first day in the gym locker room, was the leader of his own crew. Although he proudly proclaimed to be in the Junior Mexican Mafia, I'm pretty sure most of his crew was not, but he was the safest choice for them to hang out with. They were the most Mexican of the gangs and for the most part, they kept to themselves, but they noticed everything that went on. Raymond had a number two kid who was a short, chubby serious-looking, Hispanic kid. I never heard him say a word in three years, but he was always with Raymond as his quiet enforcer, ready for action.

None of Raymond's crew members were very big, which meant they had to be fiercer than the other gangs. They also did not go out of their way to cause trouble. A couple of them got *necio* or rowdy, but Raymond kept them in check because he made the rules, a young Mexican version of the Godfather.

The NDs and Raymond's crew members were all regulars who lived in the Alazán-Apache Courts.

In response to the neighborhood gangs, a group of multilingual kids formed a gang called the SOT or Studs of Tafolla, who were without a doubt the biggest troublemakers. They were posers to me because they only formed a gang to feel tough. The only reason we had to take them seriously was because there were a lot of them. They wanted to prove they were legit even though they weren't. I hated them.

They came from mostly middle-class families who learned about gangs from the movie *Colors* or *Blood In, Blood Out*. They had no real perspective about what it took to join a gang or what being in a gang meant, yet they wanted to play Crips and Bloods at school. None of them worried about where their next meal was going to come from. They did obnoxious things, and they were always looking for trouble or causing trouble. There were so many of them, they felt they had an edge. Any reason was good for starting a fight so they could prove their toughness. They were ones that really started *carrilla,* which I will explain later.

If you finished eating lunch early, which we all did, then the students left the cafeteria and most of the boys went to the basketball courts. It was far from sight of the cafeteria and the perfect setting for trouble. It was off the gym, but the NDs hung out right outside the gym, so no one approached those doors. If trouble went down, escaping was a long run to the cafeteria doors.

Not long after he introduced himself in the locker room, Raymond said to me, "Hey, you should come hang with us." I was honored and very respectful about saying, "No, no, no, I'm good. Thank you." I hadn't really found my crew yet since my few friends had a different lunch period, but at the very least, I knew I didn't have anything in common with Raymond and his crew. Unless they read Marvel or Image comics and I didn't know about it. Doubtful.

Every gang had an initiation. The initiations were simple: if you decided you wanted to join a gang, you had to get beat up by the gang members for thirty seconds or a minute. I saw it happen once. It happened behind the gym at Tafolla at lunchtime. I walked up and stumbled upon it as it was about to happen. There were about six guys all circled around a guy who was trying to be brave and hold his chin up high. The other guys were asking him if he really had what it took to be "in" and he kept saying, "*Simón, güey*." Then all of a sudden, the fists started flying. He tried to fight back but there were too many punches coming from all directions. Finally, he fell down and they proceeded to all kick him while he was down. Then it was over as quickly as it had started. It's terrifying to watch ten or fifteen people beat up one person. For a guy like that, it was worth it though. After the initiation, you were the real deal and your crew would always have your back, but for me, membership wasn't worth the price of admission.

While the potential for middle school gang violence was always there, the gang violence on the streets of my neighborhood was just as bad. The rules were the same, but the gang members were adults and actively involved in shootings. At Tafolla, the gangs were contained within four walls, but if someone assumed I had joined a gang, it would have caused trouble at home and in my neighborhood.

The Olmos Boys were the biggest threat in my neighborhood, and they seemed to love to bring old western style shootouts to our streets. They came out of nowhere and their core members lived in the two houses across the street from mine. The funny thing was Olmos is a street near my house. But most of the gang members didn't live on Olmos, they lived on my street which was Hermosa. Bunch of dumb dumbs. Our house was the last house on a dead-end part of Hermosa. The guys who lived in those houses would do a drive-by several blocks away to another gang and then there'd be retaliation drive-bys on our street. Our house, because it was next to the gang members' houses, was often in the line of fire during the retaliation drive-bys. The Olmos Boys were not a crew that I was particularly afraid of, except for this one problem: they brought flying bullets to our very doorstep.

Around this time, I realized something that gave me a tiny little peace of mind. I realized that I actually belonged to very special gang already that wasn't a gang—my brothers, the Gomez clan. I found a lot of comfort knowing that if shit ever really hit the fan, I had three older brothers, Danny, Mark, and Hector, who could hold their own. The Gomez boys weren't big, but all the stories I had ever heard were enough to make a little brother proud. All of my brothers had played football at Edison High School and each of them had their own reputation for toughness and could go all twelve rounds if they had to. My brother Mark was so exceptionally strong and good at fighting that it was as if God had taken all the power of fist-fighting for the entire Gomez family and given it to Mark. Although I never did call on them, I knew if I needed the Gomez brothers, they would have rushed to my rescue, which is probably why I never did it. If something was going to go down that required the nuclear option, there was no stopping that boulder from rolling down the hill. There would have been dead bodies everywhere.

SAFETY AND BELONGING

DEAR LENCH,

There is something that no one ever told me about being a young person that I want to explain for the first time. When you're growing up, and when you're living life, one of the very first needs a human being requires is that of safety. You need to feel physically safe in the environment that you are in. One of the other important human needs is that craving we all have for a sense of belonging.

In your story, right away, there was an unhealthy, unintended hierarchy that the school system introduced. This hierarchy made you feel both physically unsafe and desperate, looking around to see where you belonged. You and I both know that we felt different, and that was not a good thing in this brand-new environment.

Let's talk about gangs.

First of all, I'm sorry no one ever sat you down and told you that one of the things in life you would have to deal with is gangs. I'm sorry no one ever told you how scary and violent they could be.

These kids in the gangs in your neighborhood and your school were scary. You saw a lot of the bad stuff they did. You saw them shoot people, jump each other, and beat up people who didn't deserve to be beaten up. That's all true. Let me tell you what's also true. All of those kids also wanted safety, too, and they were scared.

They didn't deal with safety the way you did. You could go home. You could rest assured that Danny, Mark, and Hector would help you if they needed to. You could create safety for yourselves. Those kids couldn't, so they formed a gang to be safe.

A lot of those kids didn't have a family the way you had a family. Growing up, all the kids on Hermosa Street without a mom or dad wanted Mom and Pops to be their parents. They wanted to be part of the Gomez family; you already were.

A lot of those kids chose the gangs to be their family. It wasn't healthy but that's where they found their sense of belonging. They belonged to a family that did hurtful things, and it wasn't cool.

You belong to a family that loves you, and that's a good thing. Don't look at these kids as evil, terrible people, because they're just trying to get what you had waiting for you at home. They were still kids. They grew up on the streets, but you didn't. They were kids from San Antonio, with a mom and dad, brothers and sisters. They were in those gangs, but they also wanted to live a life of safety and belonging. Just like you.

You know what is also true? They were not all bad kids. You describe them all as gang members and troublemakers, but I want you to know that is not true. Lots of them were good kids. Some of them never got into trouble or went out of their way to get into trouble. That is also true. You just don't remember those kids because you were too busy focusing on the bad ones so you could be safe. But you can't label them all as bad, because that is not true. It's not either/or. The truth is there were bad kids AND there were also good kids. Don't tell yourself the story that everyone on the Westside was bad, because it will poison your mind.

One of the foundations of human development is the need to feel physically safe. In fact, it's the kids on the Westside who didn't know that's what was happening, but to be safe, you had to be in a gang, even if you didn't call it a gang. Nature was taking its course in which a bunch of people needed to be safe, and the number one way to be safe was to not be alone.

At the time, you felt vulnerable because you weren't part of a gang. You had no protection, and you stuck out as an easy target for them to take out whatever garbage they were dealing with. Without joining a gang, the message you sent was, "I don't belong to anyone," and maybe they translated it as, "Nobody wants that guy, so he's gotta have something wrong with him. And so it's easy for me to pick on someone that nobody wants." The truth is, you did belong, you were wanted, and there was nothing wrong with you. Don't believe the lies.

FIGHT OR FLIGHT

People deal with fear differently. In the wild, there is something called fight and flight response. It has to do with what an animal does when it's cornered by a predator. People have the same response when it comes to danger. Some people hide or run away when they feel frightened or threatened; they take flight. Some people lash out when they're afraid; they fight. Some people will hit you not because they're angry, but because on the inside they are barking like a cornered dog; they're really afraid. You need to know that a lot of these kids, even the toughest guys, were just as afraid as you were. They just dealt with their fear very differently. Some of them were so afraid that they used violence to mask their fear. Some of them would fight to make you afraid before they were afraid. Why does this matter? It matters because I need you to see these kids as people. It's easy to hate someone you can label as bad. It's harder to hate someone when you see their humanity. But you have to decide to see it, and I hope you will.

CHAPTER 3

RULES AND RITUALS

By the time January came and the second semester began, I thought I'd figured out most of the rules and rituals I had to follow to stay safe. I did my best to remain invisible, minded my own business, and didn't look at many people, especially guys bigger than me, in the eye.

By then I knew that certain places were safe—the classrooms, the principal's office, the bench outside the cafeteria—and those that weren't—the bathroom, the locker room, and any dark corners where no one could see what was happening. I thought the bus was safe, too, because each day it took us away from where all the trouble was. The problem was that sometimes trouble followed you home if you didn't watch yourself.

I'd known Daniel since elementary school. We lived in

the same neighborhood. He wasn't very tall, but he was good-looking, he had beautiful, straight, dirty blond hair that fell around his face. He looked like some sort of kid movie star and all the girls went bananas over his hair. I was jealous of the attention he got, but I had to admit he had great hair. My hair was the opposite of Daniel's. I had a cowlick on the top in front and three in the back. I couldn't get my hair to do what I wanted even if I super glued it. I think I was just jealous of Daniel's hair.

He loved to clown around and could reach a level of *necio* that I didn't think was possible. When we were in fourth grade, I left my desk for a minute to get a piece of paper. When I came back, just before I sat down, Daniel held a sharpened pencil in his fist on my seat, and I sat on it. It stabbed my right butt cheek and was one of the most painful things that had happened to me to that point. Daniel got in trouble, but he didn't get expelled, probably saved by his beautiful hair.

By the time we got to Tafolla, my butt cheek had healed, and we were pretty good friends. I'd forgiven him for stabbing me in the butt with a pencil. He was that kind of guy. He wasn't mean-spirited; he just did what he thought would be funny without thinking it might hurt someone else, and he didn't worry about getting in trouble because his looks usually saved him. By middle school, he'd become a ladies' man. He was funny, and he loved to flirt.

One afternoon at the end of the school day, the multilingual students from Whittier boarded the Route Five bus to go home, but Daniel wasn't on the bus that day. When we got off the bus at Whittier, two unfamiliar-looking guys approached us. I didn't know them but knew they weren't from the Whittier neighborhood. One of them said, "Where's Daniel?" I told them he wasn't on the bus today and asked why. One guy said, "Because I'm going to stab him. He's been flirting with my girl at Tafolla." And he showed me his knife. I said, "Well, he's not here," and walked away as quickly as I could.

I thought the bus was a safe place. I never thought that flirting with a girl could get you stabbed. I hadn't even considered this category of actions that could hurt me. I started running through a mental checklist: what girls have I been talking to? How many of them have boyfriends? How many of those boyfriends might think my talking is flirting? I did not want to get stabbed, and now I had another thing to worry about. Then I remembered that I was terrified of girls and didn't know how to talk to them. Danger avoided.

Daniel stayed safe that day, but the guy was not giving up so easily. A few days later, I saw the boyfriend with one of his buddies on the football field at Tafolla. I was skipping lunch, as usual, and so I was one of the only guys on the field walking toward the basketball courts. They spotted me immediately and the boyfriend asked, "Where's Daniel?" I said, "I don't know, probably in the cafeteria." He marched off toward the cafeteria.

I kept walking toward the courts. The school policeman, Officer Almendarez, had seen the two guys talk to me. He knew something was up and asked me, "Lorenzo, who are those guys? What are they doing here?" I knew ratting on someone was against the rules, but I also had great respect for authority, and I didn't want Daniel to get stabbed. I looked down and kept walking. I muttered, "He's here to stab Daniel because Daniel has been flirting with his girlfriend."

Officer Almendarez was a short, stocky guy. He wasn't someone that you would think was fit, yet he ran faster than I could have imagined and grabbed the boyfriend and his buddy before they reached the cafeteria. He slammed them against the wall and arrested them on the spot. All I could think was, "I hope no one saw me say what I just said, especially the guy that just got arrested. Because if he saw me, and he thinks I ratted him out, he's gonna come and stab me." I had just violated one of the rules of the street.

HAPPY BIRTHDAY TO YOU

All the gangs at Tafolla practiced something called *carrilla*, the ritual of getting jumped and beat up on your birthday. To this day, I still don't know what *carrilla* translates to, but I think it has something to do with bullying. Either way, it was a word that struck fear into the heart of every single boy at Tafolla. If someone asked when my birthday was, I made up a fake date in July, any date that wasn't during the school year. No school had ever had so many students whose birthdays were in the summer. I saw *carrilla* happen a couple times, and I knew I didn't want that gift.

The first time I witnessed *carrilla*, I was minding my business, getting ready for PE when somebody shouted, "Hey, it's Tony's birthday," and laughed in an evil sort of way. And just like, that it was on. Tony had no time to react, no time to plead his case, or think on his feet. All of a sudden ten guys jumped Tony and dragged him, with his clothes on, into the showers.

I sat near my gym locker, staring at the floor, shaking a little bit with each thud that vibrated in the tiled shower when somebody punched or kicked Tony. I felt completely helpless not knowing what I was supposed to do or not do, but I realized that having a birthday was dangerous. My whole life I thought that birthdays were something to celebrate and be happy about. Only at Tafolla could they take a birthday and make it about pain.

There was nothing I could do if ten guys wanted to drag another guy, or me, into another room and beat us up. I felt like a coward because I neither helped Tony nor joined the birthday assault. Would they think I'm a sissy because I didn't participate?

When I got home, I told my brother, Danny, the story, and he said, "Oh, yeah. That happened when I was at Edison High School. They called it 'poling' at Edison. On his birthday, a guy on the football team was jumped and dragged to the field after practice. They spread his legs and racked him on the football pole until he threw up."

I thought about Danny's story, and it became clear that getting dragged into the locker room shower and getting beaten up was not the extent of what could happen on your birthday. People were creative when it came to pain and torture. I would have picked ten guys beating me up and throwing me in the shower with my clothes on over getting racked on a pole, any day of the week.

Another time, my heart filled with pity as I saw a girl carrying a bunch of Happy Birthday balloons across the courtyard during lunch. As she walked toward her boyfriend, every single boy stopped, and silence fell as everyone turned to see who she was skipping toward. I followed her trajectory and spotted some guy I didn't know. His normally warm brown Hispanic face turned white as the blood rushed out, and like an Old Testament prophet I saw his future. I could feel his fear. It was too late for him to run, and he knew what was coming. I winced as five random guys rushed and jumped him before his birthday balloons reached his hand. The girl stopped short still holding the balloons as she slowly realized what she had done. She was in shock as her boyfriend was curled up on the floor, paying the price for her kindness. Happy Birthday, *vato*.

Only once did I see someone escape *carrilla*. The rumor that morning had been that it was Tracy's birthday. Tracy was one of two black kids in the school, and he was often teased because he had a girl's name. The thought on everyone's mind that day was, "Poor Tracy."

That day, like all the other days, during my lunch period I sat outside near the cafeteria door. An administrator stood there, so it was a safe place. The one white, curly-haired redhead kid in our school, Chuck, sat there too. He was a super smart, overweight kid, and the fact that he looked different than everyone else made him a target for teasing and bullying. He probably needed a safe place more than I did. It sucked, too, because Chuck was an awesome person.

Chuck and I were hanging out, staring at the football field, when we heard a commotion in the distance. We turned toward the noise and saw Tracy in full sprint running across the football field followed by at least twenty guys, also in full sprint.

Once again, the world turned into a slow-motion movie. Chuck and I sat in awe and watched Tracy literally running for his life. For some reason even though I saw this scene happening in slow motion, the soundtrack song to this was a fast one. As Tracy ran from the mob, the song *Jesus Built My Hotrod* by Ministry was playing in my head. I didn't listen to Ministry much, because they were super hard-core metal, and I could only take them in small doses. As I saw the most dramatic escape I have ever witnessed—to this day—the song made perfect sense. Tracy was a combination of a NASCAR hotrod and a cheetah running on the Discovery Channel. The difference, of course, was on the Discovery Channel the cheetah is chasing something; here, the cheetah was being chased. Chuck and I sat there with our mouths hanging open. Under our breath, we were rooting for him, "Go, Tracy, go, go, go." In short, Tracy smoked those fools. He finally jumped the school fence and ran all the way home. It was like watching someone break out of jail. Chuck and I did our best not to jump off the bench and cheer, because that might have meant we'd get beaten up. Tracy's escape was one of the craziest, most amazing things I'd ever seen.

QUIERES CHINGASOS?

When I was little, my family raised fighting roosters from Mexico as pets. We had a huge incubator in our kitchen, and I would stare at it for days waiting for two chicks to hatch. One day two baby fighting chicks hatched at the same time. As soon as they pecked their way out of their eggs, they looked at each other and instantly started fighting.

Adult fighting roosters were even crazier. Each of my siblings and I had a fighting rooster that was our pet, and we never wanted them hurt, but we used to let them fight. I remember Danny and Denise would hold their roosters until it was time. Then they would let them go and the roosters would instantly go at it. All you could see was a cloud of feathers. Mark was waiting with the water hose to spray them down and separate them so they wouldn't get hurt.

The *cholos* at Tafolla reminded me of those roosters.

I was shy, quiet, and spent a lot of time thinking. I'd stare into space while dreaming about the next issue of Spawn or Social Distortion's next album. One day while I was Tafolla people watching, I saw one guy looking at another guy. It seemed like he was staring into space like I was, but his gaze fell on another guy. After three seconds, the second guy said, "*Quieres chingasos?*" or "What are you staring at? Do you want to fight?"

The guy who'd been staring into space said, "What if I do?"

Faster than the words left his mouth, it went down. Just like those fighting roosters, the two *cholos* raised their heads, pulled back their shoulders to puff up their chests, and went at each other in a cloud of fists instead of feathers. It was a scene right out of the song *Insane in the Brain* by Cypress Hill.

In that moment, I realized I couldn't stare at people, whether I meant to or not. Add it to the list, I guess. When I saw that throw down, I understood that the worst thing you could be at Tafolla was a people watcher. If you stared at someone for more than three seconds, you were asking for trouble. Staring for more than three seconds always begged the question: *Quieres chingasos?*

I did the only thing I knew how to do: I looked at my feet. When I walked to my class, I went out of my way to look down. When I was in class, I looked down, especially if I scanned the room and saw gangsters or anyone I didn't know. To this day, I struggle with bad posture, probably from looking at my feet for three years in middle school. My mother would always get mad at me and tell me to straighten up. I would for a while but there was no way she was going to undo all the time I spent at Tafolla looking down.

I could have been walking with my head up, reading the posters on the walls, looking toward the classroom I had to reach, or simply looked at people, given them a fake smile, and said, "Good morning," or "Hey, what's up?" There probably wasn't retribution for asking, "What's up?" I never considered those options, though. I chose the most radical option and looked down.

Truth is, I was too afraid to converse with people I didn't know, yet, I probably would have gotten further with a quick smile. I might have made friends if I'd held my head up high and projected the message, "I'm not here to fight. Hey, what's going on?"

TAKE YOUR SEATS

In the cafeteria and on the basketball court, everyone hung with their crew, or if they weren't in a gang—like me—with the kids who were most similar. The rules changed when we stepped into the classroom. The teacher assigned seats to the students. The unspoken rule was that members of opposing gangs could be friends in the classroom if they were seated next to each other. I sat next to Sam, who was part of Raymond's crew, and he was funny. We'd laugh and joke, but as soon as we left the classroom, we once again assumed our social roles. He hung with Raymond, and I kept to myself.

In the classroom, all students had a common enemy: the teacher. In the classroom, it was us versus them. I had something in common with the guy next to me because we both thought, "This stupid teacher, making us do homework or some dumb project." No one wanted to be the teacher's pet or worse, come across as someone who snitched about what went on outside the classroom.

One time we had a substitute teacher in PE, and we were just out of control, ignoring the sub and anything he told us to do. We were playing basketball and the sub was getting angry that we wouldn't listen to him. One of the guys from the Westside turned to the sub and, in Spanish, said, "*Callate el hocico*" which means shut your animal mouth. And then told us, (in English) "Don't listen to him, *güey*. Keep playing." His move was subtle, but by using both languages, he showed the sub who was boss.

The sub gave in; what else could he do? Is his hundred dollars a day worth fighting the students on the Westside of San Antonio?

I confess I felt some inner conflict. I grew up in a household where you were told to respect adults. On the court that day, not only did we not respect them, we were insulting and ignoring them, and getting away with it. By going along with the regulars, I was suddenly in their league. It was us against the teacher. I had to choose sides: I loved learning, but I also wanted to be safe, and there was no way I was going to rat on somebody and risk getting beat up.

A "rat" was the worst thing to be called.

I did my best to keep my distance from anyone in a gang, but Tafolla was a big school, so it was inevitable that I'd have to interact with some of them sometime, and sometimes take their side, like the day with the substitute teacher. A bunch of dudes from Raymond's crew were in social studies with me. They loved to play basketball like I did, so we got along great during the class. Once we left the classroom, the joking stopped, and we went our separate ways.

Unless we were playing basketball together.

BASKETBALL

Members of different gangs could play basketball together because we only had one ball or on rare occasions two, so we had to play together. Allegiances were put on pause on the basketball court.

Most kids went outside after they finished eating lunch. I went directly outside, since I stopped eating lunch after the first day of sixth grade.

The cafeteria doors led out to the football field and a large open area. The basketball court was at the end of the campus, with buildings on three sides: the main school building on one side, and two gyms on the other sides. When we were on the basketball court at lunchtime, the sun was high, and the sky was bright. There was no hiding. The basketball court area was my version of the prison yard you see in movies.

Everybody hung out there, met with their cliques, and if a fight was going to happen, it took place there. If you wanted to talk to a girl or have a deep conversation with your buddy, you'd walk around the football field.

On a good day, lunch period was spent playing basketball without any fights. Most of the boys loved playing basketball, and some of the guys were really good.

Those of us who weren't regulars were introduced to games we'd never heard of or seen before. Some of the guys played games that made no sense and, surprise, were all designed to hurt anyone for any reason. One was called Wall Ball. The idea was that one guy had a tennis ball, which he had to throw against a wall and catch. If he caught it, everything was good. If he dropped it, he had to run and touch the wall. The other players would grab the ball and throw it at the first player as hard as possible to hit him before he touched the wall. I played once and realized how strong some people were. If you dropped the ball, some big dude could pick it up and pelt you in the back, knocking the wind out of you. I quickly set my own rule of not playing games I didn't know.

Another game designed for punishment, and terribly named, was called Smear the Queer. Someone threw a ball at another person, and if the ball hit the person, everyone else would tackle him. Some people loved playing these games; I never understood any of it.

The last rule of safety I learned was to not leave campus. The neighboring Alazán-Apache Courts public housing complex was very unsafe. In one class I sat next to a window, and every day I saw an ambulance or police car parked at the Courts—every single day. Leaving campus wasn't an option I even wanted to consider.

Two sides of the campus were surrounded by a twelve-foot-high chain-link fence. I don't know if it was meant to keep the students in or keep the people from the neighborhood out. Beyond the fence on the side with the football field was a flood drainage ditch that was usually dry and empty. When it rained, the ditch flowed with dirty brown water and debris—milk cartons, plastic bags, and once a dead body. Half a mile beyond that ditch was the county jail. It often felt like being in jail looking at another jail.

The school year ended, and I had learned the rules and rituals. I wasn't sure if seventh grade would be about learning or about trying to make friends, but I was glad a third of my middle school experience was finished.

MAKE YOUR OWN RULES

DEAR LENCH,

You know, figuring out the rules is something you are going to have to do—everywhere. When you start a job, there are certain bosses that will give you the freedom to do whatever you need to. Others will demand a play by play breakdown of everything you have done. You'll just have to learn the lay of the land, and you'll never stop. The situations get less violent for sure, but the whole notion of learning the rules and rituals will happen every place you go—every job, every community, every church. You have to learn what the unspoken rules are and always be on the lookout for them. The good news is that most of the rules won't be about who can physically hurt you and when.

Remember, the only thing you can control is you. In the face of violence and gang rituals at Tafolla, you could have made your own rules and rituals that would have been more positive to the world.

The question is: are there things that you can do? Rules and rituals that you could create, that would introduce a positive light in the world? That other people will look at and go, "Man, I want to do something like that."

Your fear made you focus on yourself and your own safety. I get it, but you could have listened to the people around you. You loved comic books. What if one of the guys in social studies had been into Wolverine, and you'd spent the two bucks to buy him a Wolverine comic book? You would have created goodwill and maybe even a friend. Your rule could have been, "I listen to people, and when an opportunity comes up for me to introduce a little goodness into the world, I give it a shot."

What if you'd started a trend of listening to the things people liked and going a little out of your way to help them. Your parents did that all the time in the neighborhood. They gave to the gang members and kids that lived nearby, and that's one of the reasons your parents were beloved in our neighborhood.

I know why you didn't do any of these things. In your fear, you shut down and stopped looking outward. When you hold on to your fear, it blinds you. It clouds your vision. You forget about the people around you. Then fear becomes anger, and it's easier to hate someone than to help them.

But there is the problem. I think Keller once said that in order to hate someone, you must first convince yourself that you are better than they are. You were not better than anyone else. You were all struggling with the same stuff and you all choose to handle it differently.

Your family had rules and rituals for helping people. Your parents prayed for anyone who needed help and set a great example for you. You've seen them visit hospitals, prisons, and funeral homes on their quest to help anyone in need.

Sometimes helping people is the most gangster thing you can do. It's how the Godfather actually got all his power, by doing favors and helping people. Just don't do the rest of the stuff he did.

So what's my point? My point is that you can decide to set your own rules and rituals. And they can be forces for good. Do it your own way, but it requires you to be looking out for people to help.

And because so few people do it in this world, it's actually the most punk rock thing you can do.

CHAPTER 4

~~~~~~~~~

A SUMMER OF DRIVE-BYS

Tio Mongui was one of my mom's fifteen siblings. He had a larger-than-life personality, and every time he walked into the room, everybody laughed a little harder and smiled a little bigger. My mom once told me that in all matters of macho toughness, her brother Mongui was the leader.

One of my older siblings once told me a story about my mother's brothers that to this day reminds me of a movie. A long time ago, before I was born, my family was visiting our Grandma Petra in Laredo. They often went to visit, but this time something was different. At that time another uncle, Tio Riche, was doing time in a Mexican prison across the river from Laredo. The prison was called

La Loma, which means "The Hill" in Spanish. As soon as my parents and siblings walked into my Grandma Petra's house, they saw all of my mother's brothers gathered in the house, and every single one of them was loading guns with bullets. As night fell, they all left and went across the border to pay a little visit to La Loma where their brother was.

The very next morning when my siblings woke up for breakfast, they walked into my Grandma's kitchen and found Tio Riche quietly sitting at the table having coffee with my grandma. I wasn't alive when this happened, but I loved that story as if I had found Tio Riche in the kitchen drinking coffee. Every time I saw Tio Mongui with his macho, larger-than-life personality, I imagined that he was the one who led the charge.

Needless to say, my mom's side of the family is the colorful part. Tio Mongui was beloved by my mother and my whole family. He was married and had two daughters and a son who was my age. We played together a lot, so I saw Tio Mongui a lot, too. He used to call me Rambo, because when I was five years old, I was obsessed with the movie *Rambo* and liked to dress in camouflage.

It could've been Tio Mongui's handsome looks that got him into trouble. He had a well-groomed mustache and wore cowboy boots and a cowboy hat in typical Laredo style. He was tall and took long, slow strides, as if to say, "I don't have to hurry for anyone."

It could've been Tio Mongui's success that got him into trouble. He ran a successful bail bonds company. He was the first entrepreneur I knew and the first person I saw carrying a cell phone, back when cell phones were the size of bricks and only celebrities or very rich people could afford one. His brick of a cell phone hung like a pistol from his leather belt and swung back and forth as he walked.

In the end, it was Tio Mongui's generous heart that got him into trouble. The city of Laredo is split between Texas and Mexico; the border between the United States and Mexico is literally divided by the Rio Grande River. A man in Laredo, Texas, killed two brothers across the river in Mexico. The killer returned to the Texas side and the US authorities picked him up for stealing a car and put him in jail. He knew the family of the dead brothers would find him there and come to kill him.

The killer's mother was my uncle's neighbor. He was her third and only surviving son, so even though he was a killer, he was all she had. She went to my Tio Mongui and begged him to bail her son out of jail. My uncle was not stupid; he knew the other family was looking for this guy, but my uncle's heart was bigger than his fear. When the sweet mother came and begged my uncle for help to keep her son alive, he didn't know how to say no.

Even as a twelve-year-old, I knew he shouldn't bail the guy out, but life is complicated. All of my memories of Laredo were of my loving, caring, and hospitable family. They cooked, they cleaned, they did whatever they could for their family, they would give you the shirt off their back. They would let you move into the back room if you didn't have a place to stay. They were really loving, generous people.

I imagine this guy's mom pleading to my uncle. I imagined her as one of my aunts or my grandma. I put myself in my uncle's shoes and thought if one of my aunts or grandmas came begging and pleading, I would absolutely not be able to tell them no. The characters in Laredo were so pure, loving, and giving that you couldn't say no to them, much less one that was begging, crying, and pleading for the life of her son.

When the family of the murdered brothers in Mexico learned that my uncle had posted the bail bond to free the killer, they said, "We're gonna kill that guy, and one of his brothers, so they know what it feels like." Word spread fast across the border between Mexico and Texas.

On February 26, I got off the bus and walked toward my

house as I did on most days after school. I was within three houses of mine when I saw people outside on the porch crying. I knew something was wrong. I ran up the front steps, asking, "What happened?" My brothers and mother repeated the same words simultaneously, "They killed Mongui. They murdered him. They shot him." My mom was hysterical. Her beloved brother had been murdered. Before that day, I had never known anyone who had died. That day I wished that I still didn't. I wished that if I was going to know someone that had died it wouldn't be someone in my family. And I wished most of all that it wasn't someone that my mom loved so very much.

My uncle was having lunch with some relatives when he got a call to meet an acquaintance at the Civic Center parking lot, which is really close to my grandma's house. When he drove up, the acquaintance got in the truck, pulled out a gun, and said, "We're gonna go for a drive." The plan was to drive to the river and make my uncle call his brother to meet him at the river, and then both my uncles would be killed. On the way, my uncle intentionally crashed his truck into a fence, and the man shot my uncle six times, leaving him to bleed to death in the cab of his truck. My uncle managed to send a coded 911 message to his brother and save his life.

His brother, Vito, my other uncle, is a lawyer and was in court that day. As soon as he received the coded message, he ran out of the courtroom to help his brother, but it was too late. He received a call from the chief of police, who was a friend of his. The chief said, "They killed your brother. We need you to come identify the body."

My Tio Vito identified the body for the police, then turned away and cried. The next day, the local newspaper ran a photo of Vito turning from the truck and that image is embedded in my memory to this day.

My uncle's murder was my first true confrontation with death. I saw people I loved behave in ways I'd never seen before.

The other family never killed my Tio Vito, and one of my family legends is that my other uncles went into Mexico and wreaked havoc, taking revenge for my uncle's murder and doing things too terrible to write about here.

At my uncle's funeral, my Grandma Petra, who was the Jaime family's pillar of strength, cried hysterically as she walked from the entrance of the church to the casket, screaming in Spanish all the baby nicknames she had for my uncle. I had never seen my grandma behave this way, nor ever seen anything like this event.

My Tio Riche, who was so tough he survived a Mexican prison and prison break, refused to attend the funeral. I always wondered how I would have reacted if I were in his shoes. My brother later told me that Tio Riche didn't attend any funerals at all, which I thought was weird and confusing. I walked up to the casket to pay my last respects. I noticed the morticians had done as good a job as they could to hide the bullet holes with makeup, but I could still see some of them. In that moment, I realized my uncle was dead and not coming back. He did what he thought was a good thing, helping an elderly mother save her son, and paid for it with his own life.

I was afraid of school and I was afraid of my neighborhood. Now, the reality that murder was not just something you saw in movies haunted me. For years to come, the memory of Tio Mongui would live on. At every family wedding the *mariachis* would play the classics. But every time they played the song *El Rey*, all my aunts would lose it and start crying. They would sing along, crying while holding their chests tight, and after they would tell us that it was Tio Mongui's favorite song. *El Rey* means "The King."

ESCALATING VIOLENCE

The summer after sixth grade began under the cloud of my uncle's murder. There were 3.5 drive-by shootings on average every day that year in San Antonio, Texas. My neighbors, Joelle, Noelle, and Oscar, were part of the gang violence, so it often came close to our home.

The gang violence had escalated but also become so commonplace that some days we didn't notice it. One day I was talking on the phone with my friend Joe, and I heard the popping sound of gunfire. I said, "Hey, Joe, hang on for a second," while I grabbed the phone cord and moved to sit with my back to a wall, which was the safest place to sit when there's gunfire. Who knows if that is true but that is what I told myself. They don't teach you drive-by safety in school, so I just did what I saw people do during shootouts in the movies. We then carried on with our conversation—while the drive-by was happening.

Another time, Joe and I were on the phone and could hear the same drive-by even though we lived on opposite sides of Interstate 10. We tried to figure out which street it was on based on the direction we could hear the shots coming from. Most drive-bys didn't sound like gunshots in a movie. Shotguns had a slow, loud boom. A handgun or rifle made pop-pop sounds. This was the first and only time I'd heard gunshots like what I'd heard in a *Die Hard* movie: this was a machine gun. It was fast and staccato. "I guess they got some upgrades," Joe said.

The irony is crazy. Every day for the past school year, I had lived in fear of being beaten up at school, but I was completely desensitized to drive-by shootings. Kids in my neighborhood were desensitized to all kinds of horrific circumstances. I knew a bunch of kids whose families sold drugs or did drugs in front of them. Other kids lived with parents who fought violently all the time.

The violence didn't end with drive-by shootings. One night my whole family was sleeping and without warning, everyone was up and talking loud and fast, running into my sister Sonia's room on the other side of the house from the bedroom I shared with my brothers. I walked in and over their voices, I could hear a crackling noise. The night was bright outside her window. A car was burning in a full blaze across the street and we simply watched, like we would have watched the fireworks on Fourth of July—but with less enthusiasm, because my reaction was nothing more than, "Oh."

We never knew the story behind the burning car. We assumed someone had stolen it, abandoned it on our street, and set it on fire. Maybe they wanted to hide evidence of a greater crime or maybe it was an act of a pyromaniac. We never did find out.

During this season the Olmos Boys went into overdrive. They started going to parties and picking fights, or whatever gangs do in their spare time, and it was pissing a bunch of people off. The retaliation drive-bys in our neighborhood seemed to go from zero to ten. When my mom was cooking, she could see the Olmos Boys' houses outside the kitchen window. Our neighbor Elise also lived across the street from the gang members' home. Elise would call my mom, and say, "Sylvia, I see you cooking, and I just heard from my son that the boys across the street just did a shooting, so there's going to be a drive-by. You need to stop cooking and get away from the window because they are heading over here now to shoot back at them."

Elise's sons were friends with the gang members, but they weren't in the gang, and so they had all this information. At times, one of the mothers of the gang members would say to Elise, "My son and those guys just shot up a house. This is what's happening." For as violent as the gangs were, they would warn their mothers to get to the very back of the house and the network of mothers would warn each other.

We would always get tip offs, and my mom seemed unafraid. I felt safe being near her, which is probably why I could nonchalantly continue my phone call with Joe during a drive-by shooting.

Mom would call the cops and tell them everything she knew, what they looked like, the weapons they had. She could see their activity from our kitchen window. One time there was a gang meeting right in their front yard. They got tipped off that there was a raid coming and they threw all their guns into the bushes nearby. When the cops came, my mom was on the phone literally during the raid telling the police where the gang members threw the guns.

The scariest moment happened that summer between sixth and seventh grade. It was about six in the evening and the sky was dark, like a storm was brewing. Elise called Mom to tell her a drive-by was going to happen. Not two minutes later, six dudes walked down our street openly carrying shotguns and pistols. It was something out of *Tombstone*. Mom stood in the window with the curtains drawn and described the men to the cops while they walked by. My sisters and I screamed at Mom, "They're going to see you! Close the curtain! Get away from the window! They're going to shoot us!" We were petrified, screaming, almost crying, begging her.

Mom didn't flinch. She pulled the curtain back with her right hand and held the phone to her ear with her left. We pleaded and warned, "Mom, they're going to shoot you."

She turned and said, "No, they're not. The Lord will protect me." And then continued to talk to the police. Those six guys emptied their guns into the neighbor's house and sure enough, not a single bullet came our way. I guess Mom was right, the Lord did protect us.

You'd think with all the danger in the neighborhood

I'd never leave the house, but I did. It was a boiling hot summer day like those that only happen in Texas. I was addicted to Sunkist that summer and had to have one. We'd received warning about a drive-by that was going down. We were on high alert, but I wanted my Sunkist. I walked to the convenience store a block from our house. Picnic Foods had everything a young Hispanic boy could want: sour pickles, Mexican candy, and Sunkist.

Whenever I walked to Picnic Foods, I crossed the street on the side that was farthest from the Olmos Boys' house. That particular day, a car was coming so I crossed the street quickly in front of their house. I was walking toward Picnic Foods as a brown van pulled up next to me and screeched to a halt. The window lowered, the barrel of a rifle appeared, and the shooting began. Time stopped.

I'd memorized the PSA announcements to stop, drop, and roll if there's fire. It was the only safety instruction I'd ever heard. I was standing when the van pulled up and all my reflexes froze. I looked down, closed my eyes, clenched my fists, and just stood there paralyzed, trying to make myself invisible. I could feel the vibration of the bullets as they passed in front of me and over my head. They weren't shooting at me, but they were shooting at the house I happened to be standing in front of.

After what seemed like forever, I opened my eyes and

saw my neighbor's house getting shot up. I saw my other neighbor crawling out of the back window of his house, holding a shotgun. At that moment, my fight or flight instinct spoke very clearly to me and said, "You need to get the hell out of here, dude."

I turned around and ran home. Elise saw the whole thing and to this day still tells my mom that she doesn't understand how I didn't get shot. I was literally in the crossfire. Regardless, that drive-by gave me a whole new appreciation for Pearl Jam's song *Alive*.

For a short time after that, my parents looked for a house in a different neighborhood, but all the houses they could afford were in even worse neighborhoods. Toward the end of the summer, the police set up a mobile unit in the St. Mary Magdalene Church parking lot near our home. One of the officers told my mom that our neighborhood was the second hottest spot for drive-bys in San Antonio. I don't know why but I was a little proud when my mom told me that. Everyone wants to be on a winning team, I guess.

When I wasn't avoiding drive-by shootings that summer, I worked with Pops and my other brothers. Mom and Pops had moved to San Antonio from Laredo so he could be an x-ray technician, but in his free time he built homes. I don't mean he flipped homes; he built them. He would buy an empty lot, get my brothers and me out there, and we would build the damn thing from the ground up. To us, renovating an existing house was for sissies. Pops loved the work, and it came naturally to him. I hated the work. I didn't understand the concepts, and I would often get frustrated while he was explaining them to me. My biggest gripe, however, was that my three brothers and I never had the tools to do our job. Say the job was hammering all the sheetrock in a room. There were two and a half hammers for four of us: two full hammers, a hammer with a broken handle—so you would have to hold the metal prong opposite the hammer head—and then one person just had to figure out how to nail without a hammer. Was it too much of a hassle to get four working hammers?

We built a lot of houses, and they all had post-hole foundations. We dug every single five-foot hole, but again, we didn't have four shovels. One of us had a shovel, one of us had a post-hole digger, one of us wet the ground to make digging easier because Texas soil is rocky, and the fourth person had a metal spike. As both the smallest and youngest, it was not my place to question the logic behind this strategy, but I would often wonder, "Why can't we all just have shovels so we can each dig one hole?" But nobody likes a whiner, so I kept my mouth shut.

I was so busy, I couldn't think about other things and

I suppose that was a good thing. Pops wanted us to do something productive until the school year began again. Pops was no fool, and he knew that to have four bored boys would lead to a lot of trouble.

There is a famous story in my family that happened one Christmas Day when I was still too young to pick up a hammer. After all the presents had been opened and the turkey was eaten, my brothers made a big mistake. They started complaining about being bored. Pops wasted no time curing this disease and made them all reroof the neighbor's house, which we owned but rented to a family. No one ever complained of being bored ever again.

FREE WILL, GRIEF, AND BRAVERY

DEAR LENCH,

Let's call this time of your life the Cruel Rite of Passage. Nothing has started changing physically for you, but inside your head, everything's changing. You're starting to see and feel the world around you in a different way.

Maybe you're starting to figure out that life is complicated. Until now, things seemed black and white, people were either good or bad, and you're starting to think maybe that's not always the case. When Tio Mongui was shot, for the very first time you realized that the world is not black and white.

Life rarely is. The world isn't a game or movie of cops and robbers. You need to be aware that there's way more color out there in the world than you thought there was. And sometimes bad things happen to good people, and sometimes bad people get away with doing a bad thing.

You're probably going to grapple with this notion for the rest of your life. It's something you'll think about time and again. Just when you've marinated on it for a while and think you have an answer, something will happen to make you start grappling again. Sorry, little bro.

Mom and Pops gave you the gift of a spiritual foundation, and even though there were plenty of times you didn't want to go to church or you were tired of listening to Jesus stories, those lessons gave you a guide to think about these things. You've been in church your whole life and you believe in God. The problem with this story is that God can't give you the free will to make your own choices and then control what you do. If a bad person has free will and chooses to kill someone, God can't stop them. Bad things happen in the world when the God you believe in gives people free will to do what they want to do. It's a double-edged sword of living in a world with other people.

Think of Job—talk about bad things happening to good people. He was minding his own business, living a good, faithful life, then God let the devil mess with him. All of Job's children died, he lost all his material possessions, and he was struck by illness, but he never blamed God, and he remained faithful. When Job had been stripped of everything but his life and still remained faithful, God restored his family, his health, and his wealth two-fold. It's hard for us to make sense of that story. Why did my one uncle, who always helped people, get shot, and so many other bad people live? It's still hard for me to make sense of that story, too.

Sometimes you just need to sit in silence and chew on the fact that we may never get the answer to that question. It's not fair. It's not cool. It sucks, and it's even a little bit scary. You need to know that you shouldn't stop doing good, and you shouldn't give up hope because there are bad people in the world. You do need to take the time to grieve your losses.

Nobody talks about grieving. It's an abstract concept. When you saw Grandma Petra and all the tias fall apart at the funeral, they were grieving. You were witnessing people in your family behaving in a way you'd never seen before. Their grief probably added to the shock you felt over what happened to Tio. Nobody tells you when you're young that you can grieve. If anything, we don't grieve enough. It's okay to grieve for seemingly small losses: it's okay to cry when you switch schools and recognize that you're sad because you're leaving friends and teachers behind whom you love and who love you.

If your best friend moves, it's okay to grieve. People will tell you to "man up and move on." That is actually not helpful, and anyone telling you that probably doesn't know how to grieve anyway so don't listen to them.

Now let's talk about bravery and courage. Remember your favorite stories in the Old Testament: David and Goliath, and the three Hebrew children getting thrown in the fiery furnace.

You think bravery is David running up to the giant and knocking him out with a slingshot. That's not bravery. The reason it's not bravery is because when we read the story, we expect him to win and come out on top.

Bravery is the three Hebrew children saying, "We're going to do the right thing even though we know we're probably going to die." That's what real bravery is. When Mom called the cops and said, "The Lord is going to protect me," she said that to make you feel safe, but she knew she might get shot—that's bravery.

Bravery is doing the right thing even when you know you might die.

You were afraid every day in sixth grade, but compared to your neighborhood, Tafolla wasn't so scary. You didn't risk getting shot at Tafolla, but that was a real possibility in your neighborhood.

You hated working with Pops in the summer, but you were directly contributing to your family's financial progress. All the buildings you built were rented to poor families. Mom and Pops helped build the fabric of the neighborhood, because they had to interview people, and Mom and Pops rented to people who were poor but good. Little by little, they made the neighborhood better by renting to people who were trying to work hard themselves, even though they're in the same income bracket that you were.

Mom and Pops built a legacy in the neighborhood that went beyond the violence. The love and care they have given to the neighborhood have outlasted any of the gang activity or shootings, over time. Love is stronger than violence. And in the love department, Mom and Pops are more powerful than the Godfather himself, Vito Corleone.

Even Tio Mongiu did the right thing. He knew that those brothers would want to hurt him, and he did the right thing anyway. That is bravery. He was trying to help a mother save her son, and it got him murdered, but he was going to do the right thing no matter the cost. In this cruel rite of passage, you learn that not all stories have happy endings, that even redemption can cost you everything. Adults don't tell you that life isn't fair; you learn it on your own when the time is right. One day you're a naïve little kid, and the next day a brutal thing happens, and you're hit with the full brunt of the tension of life.

Life doesn't come around and give you closure and say, "Oh, it all worked out in the end." Sometimes, life doesn't offer explanations. And in this case, Lench, neither can I. Part of being a healthy adult is accepting that we will not have all the answers and that is okay. And anyone that tells you they do have all the answers is full of crap.

Remember that.

CHAPTER 5

~~~~~~~

SMELLS LIKE TEEN ANGST

Miss Carter came to Tafolla fresh from college. It was her first year of teaching. No doubt she knew Latin; it ran in her blood. She could break down sentences with her eyes closed, but she had no training or experience for teaching in the maximum-security middle school. As a student, Latin class became the safe place for us, but I don't know how safe it was for Miss Carter. She was not prepared for us, and before long we could tell that while she was a master of Latin, she had no idea how to impose law and order in a classroom. We took over.

Considering all the other cool languages you could study at Tafolla, it's weird and surprising that I wasn't the only student in the Latin class. I have no idea how my classmates chose Latin or if they were forced to take it by other grammar-loving mothers. However they got there, I'm glad they did, because I met my best friends at Tafolla in Latin class.

We were all readers. We loved the same kind of music and movies. We had similar interests and started to cross-pollinate. If one of us was reading Marvel Comics and another read Image Comics, we compared the heroes and villains and swapped comic books. We listened to punk, metal, and grunge music and introduced each other to our personal favorite bands, like Green Day and Weezer. We watched Quentin Tarantino movies. In an environment where most kids were looking for the next fight, we were good boys trying to survive middle school. None of us wanted to join any of the gangs at Tafolla and that's what brought us together: Big Mac, Martin, Daniel, Ivan, Kevin, Joe, and me. There were others but these were the guys I felt closest to. A couple of the guys weren't in Latin but were good friends of somebody in Latin, so we let them into our non-gang.

By seventh grade, we knew all the rules. We no longer stared at or bumped into someone who would kick our butts. We didn't go to any of the unsafe places—the bathroom especially—alone. We could let our guard down a little bit because we had our crew and we inherently knew how to act.

By seventh grade, Miss Carter had surrendered her authority in Latin class. She had about ten minutes of control and then we did whatever we wanted. We read comic books, we listened to music. We brought in gaming consoles and had a video game tournament. It was crazy—I played Mortal Combat on a Sega Genesis for the first time ever in Latin class.

Big Mac and Martin had a weightlifting competition using me as the weight. Big Mac put his left hand under my neck and his right hand under my thigh, and I was bench pressed in Miss Carter's class.

Pandemonium really struck when Daniel and another guy had a wrestling match. Daniel got flipped and dropped on his head, and we thought he was gonna die. He was totally fine, but our shouts and screams when his head hit the dirty carpet floor brought the Spanish teacher from across the hall to our classroom. She barged in, staring lasers at Miss Carter, then screamed at us and stormed out. We were terrified and for five minutes, we were well-behaved.

To her credit, Miss Carter was persistent. Some teachers would have sat back and read the newspaper or written a novel while we acted like hooligans. Miss Carter instead made an effort. She would spend five to ten minutes with each of us alone and work through flashcards, trying to force the genitive or nominative case into our brains.

One time she pulled me aside and said, "Lorenzo, we're doing vocabulary." I wasn't really paying attention, and we came to a word I didn't remember. Miss Carter said, "It's your favorite Helmet song." The Latin word was "interim," which means "meantime," and that was a song from Helmet, which was one of my favorite bands at the time. I would sing the song every time I saw the word. Miss Carter thought *In The Meantime* was my favorite Helmet song; it wasn't true, but I didn't want to correct her. If I had been bolder, I would have told her that everyone knew that Helmet's greatest song was called *Unsung*. And that if the god of war, Mars, himself was going to come down from Mt. Olympus and smite all the world, he would have played Helmet's song *Unsung* while getting ready to open a can of whoop ass on everyone.

We were maniacs, yet she wanted us to learn this subject that she loved. She did what she could to get us to learn a little bit of Latin.

MY CREW

In all there were probably twenty kids in Latin class, but our core group ruled the room. There was a group of girls who sat in the back and tried to study and talk about boys while they tolerated our shenanigans. Except for Daniel with his beautiful hair, we weren't cool ladies' men; we were grungy and weird to everyone but ourselves.

BIG MAC

Big Mac got his name because he was the biggest guy in all of Tafolla. He was a middle school student with a man's body. He stood six feet three inches and weighed about three hundred pounds. I was short and skinny, about seventy-five pounds in middle school. I thought it was cool that the biggest kid in the whole school was my friend. I might have been afraid of him if we weren't friends, but he was the opposite of a gangster. Big Mac was as intelligent as anyone I knew. He loved Tarantino movies and he really loved a band called Gwar that I never got into. He was a big video game guy, and he owned the Sega Genesis that we used to play in Latin class.

One day, Big Mac rode the Route Five bus and came home with me to hang out. He didn't live in my neighborhood, and I was so happy to bring a friend home, which was very rare for me. We walked home from Whittier, stopping at Picnic Foods on the way. I got a twelve-ounce Sunkist and he got a three-liter Coke. We walked down the street like Arnold Schwarzenegger and Danny DeVito in the movie *Twins*, Big Mac drinking his three-liter soda and me with my normal twelve-ounce cup.

Big Mac never mentioned his father, and I think he lived with his mom. I only met her once when she came to Tafolla to bring Big Mac some tacos, a lot of tacos. She was so nice, and I remember being so envious—I thought

I was used to skipping lunch every day, but watching him eat those tacos made me reconsider my choice, until I remembered the bathrooms.

Coming to my house was a completely different experience. Ours was a "family unit." We ate dinner at a certain time. We would pray over dinner. My parents were always very nice to my friends, although I always warned them they'd hear about Jesus from Mom and Pops. My friends didn't care; they were always excited to come spend the night with me because my family, especially my parents, would treat them like their own children.

MARTIN

Martin was into the hardest of the hard heavy metal, but he was the only dude in Latin class who read books, thick novels by Dean Koontz. I'd see him and think, "I could never finish a book that big." Because he read so much, he had an extensive vocabulary and was super-intelligent. At thirteen, he looked like he was twenty-six, and he carried himself with confidence.

One day during the lunch period, Martin was walking across the football field to our spot at the back of the basketball court. It was a slow day at Tafolla, so to drum up some action somebody said, "Hey, it's Martin's birthday" even though it wasn't. Martin turned to look at the twelve guys coming toward him and said, "So what if it is?" And just like that the ritual of *carrilla* began. They ran straight at him, and once again my world went into slow motion. Martin squared up to them like a he was a bull in a corral, cocked back his fist, and swung so hard I could see him grinding his teeth. He only had time to get in one swing, but it was enough to make him a badass for life. With one punch he knocked down three guys. I had never seen anything like that and still have not since. The other nine jumped him, then another five piled on. From a distance I saw a horde of dudes on top of Martin, punching and kicking him. Then, in the middle of dust and beatdown, I saw a single Nike high-top go flying about thirty feet in the air, and it was over.

Back in class, Martin giggled about how he took down at least three of them. His spirit could not be broken. I was shocked that he was unphased, unchanged, and unafraid. He was my hero.

IVAN

Ivan was truly the first person I ever met that embodied the punk rock spirit. He was the first person I ever saw get a mohawk and dye his hair green. If punk rock was a video game, we were all on level one and Ivan was on level ten. He was super smart, funny, handsome—maybe not as handsome as Daniel—and the first person I saw wearing Doc Marten boots. I had one class with Ivan and that is where we became friends. I remember him being funny without being the class clown. I also saw him be kind and thoughtful when it came to the regulars in class; he never talked down to them, and he was quick to help if they asked for help with classwork. That always stuck out to me. I never expected him to be a fighter and, boy, was I wrong. I remember the first day he got into a fight. Some *cholo* regular came up to him and clearly wanted to throw down and thought Ivan was an easy target. The guy came right up in Ivan's face and started talking trash about something Ivan supposedly did that wasn't true. Ivan tried to explain the truth, but the guy was having none of it. Then I saw the switch flip in Ivan's eyes. He suddenly turned on the street fighter in him, looked the guy in the eye, and said, "So what if I did?" At Tafolla that translated to, "Let's dance, asshole." They both got so close to each other they could have been kissing. Then one of them pushed the other, and it was on like Donkey Kong. And that was the day I learned that a guy with punk rock in his heart and Doc Martens on his feet was as deadly as any Westside gangster. Ivan kicked the shit piss out of that regular's ass so much that not even the guy's friends wanted to jump in. That day I bought a ticket to ManCrushVille where Ivan was the mayor.

My brother Danny had always told me that a real fight was not like the movies. He told me that when two guys hit each other, it doesn't sound like the movies. It sounds like punching meat the way you would punch a piece of steak. That fight with Ivan is when that principle came to life for me.

Ivan and I had become good friends. One day he decided he wanted to experience my family, so he came over to spend the night. Halfway through the night, everyone went off to do their thing after we ate dinner together. Ivan looked at me and said, "It's so weird man, your family, like, gets along with each other. And it's like they like each other." Hearing his words kind of broke my heart. Even though he said it as a joke, I could tell he was dead serious.

Ivan never talked about his home life, and I can only imagine what it was like. I'm pretty sure he had to take care of himself, maybe even cook his own meals, and find his own way to school. I doubt someone helped him with his homework. He was already an adult at thirteen years old. If it's possible for a thirteen-year-old to look up to another thirteen-year-old, it happened to me. Ivan inspired me because he was alone in his world and he was making it happen.

MY FAMILY

My life was completely different. My house was full of

people. My family wasn't perfect, but we had a lot of inside jokes, a lot of love, and a lot of food. Mom only knew how to cook for at least nine people. Every meal was like Thanksgiving at my house, lots of homemade food and Pops at the head of the table, a quiet pillar maintaining order and calm. There was no craziness and shouting at our table. We had rules to follow.

As much as I said I hated the rules and structure, they were a bit part of the safety I felt in my home. I knew where and when I was going to eat, drink, and play games, and it would all be good. The stability and structure were the allure of coming to my house; we had a safe place that most of my friends didn't have.

I felt guilty because I didn't appreciate what I had. My parents were strict, so my options for hanging out and being a kid were limited. I wasn't allowed to go anywhere beyond Picnic Foods. My friends who came from less-structured families had a freedom that I didn't have. I don't know that I would have traded my secure, strict family for their freedom.

Aside from their generous nature, my parents invited my friends to our home so they could see who I was hanging out with. I'm sure they listened closely to our conversations and asked my friends about their parents. I was too self-absorbed to notice, but I have no doubt they were looking out for me. After they met some of my friends, they understood that we weren't looking for trouble. My parents loosened up a little bit and allowed me to go out with my friends.

DIVERSIONS AND ARBY'S

There was one season they let me go to a video game arcade called Diversions that was close to my house, on Fredericksburg Road. I had a taste of that freedom, and it was so much fun to hang out with some of my crew, Big Mac, Ivan, Joe, and Daniel. After the arcade we went to Arby's and bought the Five-for-Five—five sandwiches for five dollars. It was one of the greatest kid experiences I'd known, and I thought, "This is what it's like to go out and party." It wasn't the arcade or the Arby's sandwich, but the group itself and the bond we had. It was weird and special to be together outside of Tafolla. We all hated Tafolla, so having good memories of being at my house or the arcade together gave us a positive thing to bond over, too.

ALTERNATIVE TASTES

The years of our middle school happened right when there was an explosion of new music called Alternative Grunge. There was some city we had never heard of called Seattle, and it was the capital of all things grunge and alternative. Our crew loved grunge, punk, and heavy metal. But we also loved video games, comic books, and movies. We stood out because we wanted to listen to stuff that wasn't popular to everyone else. We loved talking about them, finding out about new bands or movies, and trying to convince each other that our favorite was best. With these friends, I started developing my own tastes. My dad always used to say that whoever and however your friends are will influence you. This is the main area of my life where my friends had a huge influence on me, and I loved it. It was the stuff that made me feel special and unique.

Every weekend near my house there was a huge flea market that had a few tables with a great selection of comic books. I'd go to the flea market and buy comic books, and I still have every single one of them. During that time Marvel was very popular, but I was too alternative for that. I discovered another company that made comics called Image, and their most popular comic was Spawn. It was about a CIA agent who gets killed on a mission, goes to Hell, makes a deal with the devil, and comes back to earth to see his wife and kid. But now he's loaded with tons of superpowers. I also loved Wolverine and X-men like everyone else, but there was something about Spawn. I think it's the fact that the main character was a black guy who became a superhero. It kinda made me think I could be a superhero too. I'd take my comics to Latin class, and we'd compare the skills of Spawn and Wolverine.

It was from this group of guys that I first heard about Quentin Tarantino. I saw *Reservoir Dogs* and was hooked. *Pulp Fiction* came out that year, and Joe and I went to see it. I came home traumatized by the scene where one guy rapes another guy. I was thirteen and probably shouldn't have been going to see *Pulp Fiction*. When I came home, I sat at the kitchen table and stared for what felt like an hour. I was so angry that Tarantino was allowed to put a scene like that in a film. I was so upset that I'd seen it.

I now had one more thing to fear. Was someone going to drag me into a dark corner and do that to me?

Big Mac, Joe, Martin, our other friend Kevin, and I were in PE class sitting on the bleachers. We were already starting to feel the tension of all the other gangs, and the troublemakers from the other gangs, and we hated it. We thought gangs were stupid and their names were stupid. As a joke we said we should give ourselves a name, and someone said, "Yeah, we should be the Cool Flannel Club," because we all wore flannel shirts. We could barely stop laughing because of how stupid it sounded. Someone else said, "Yeah, CFC." Then Big Mac started laughing to himself and said, "No, no, no. Change the C to a K. We'll be the KFCs," and we all almost fell off the bleachers we were laughing so hard.

Our joke took off. Other gangs would say, "I hear you guys are called KFC." And the regulars thought we were stupid because they believed we'd named our non-gang after Kentucky Fried Chicken. They had no idea we were mocking the whole gang culture. Or maybe they did, because once we became official with a name, we started getting picked on by the other gangs. By formalizing, we gave people a reason to mess with us, which was the last thing we wanted.

NO ONE IS YOU AND THAT IS AMAZING

DEAR LENCH,

So many people in the world live a double life, and you and I are no exception. You used to see this the most at church. Where people would walk in on Sunday, pretend they were perfect angels, and then raise hell every other day of the week. When you take this to the extreme, you end up acting just like in a movie. Only the movie is your real life. You start suppressing your personality and denying the things that make your personality special.

Here is my point. No one tells you this outright when you're growing up, but you need to know this now:

It is okay to be who you are.

You have certain personality traits that make you special and certain unique abilities that other people don't have. These are your God-given superpowers and they should be celebrated, not hidden from the world.

Here is an example. As you got older, all the church-going people really got into Christian music. But for some reason you didn't like it. You loved the music you loved because it spoke to you and because you loved the tension it had in it. You developed your own unique taste in music and that is part of what makes you special.

You loved the KFC crew because they were the first people at Tafolla that were okay with you being who you were. And in return you loved what made them uniquely them. This is no small thing.

As you grow up, the world is going to try to change your personality, but don't you dare let them. It's going to tell you BS like, "Adults don't do stuff like that." If you like to sing in the shower, then damn it, you sing your heart out. Your sense of humor, your love of stories, and your giggle are all part of the masterpiece that is you.

But the most important part of this principle is that you need to pass this on to the people around you who need this encouragement. I wish I could have told Martin how much I admired his reading when some could have said it was nerdy. I wish I could have told Daniel how much I loved his humor when some would have called it childish. You will meet people on your journey that stand out like sore thumbs because their personalities are shining as bright as supernovas. This is your chance to pay it forward.

Tell them you love them for who they are. Who knows, you may be the only person that has ever told them that.

CHAPTER 6

~~~~~~

ADULT SUPERVISION

Riding the Route Five bus to Tafolla each day was special to me. It was one of the few things in my life that I would call "fancy." Because Tafolla's multilingual program was such a new thing for the city, they gave it little more attention than other programs. One of them was the bus. Most kids that take a bus to school take the long yellow banana bus, but not us. All of the multilingual students got picked up by brand new buses that were used by the city's main bus system, VIA Metropolitan Transit. These buses were fancy, modern, and somehow made me feel safer. So it didn't matter if your house was falling apart, if your neighborhood sucked. 'Cause every day when Joe, Daniel, and I got to Whittier, we knew it was only a matter of time before a fancy new bus with working AC would pull up, ready to take us to school in style.

"Mornin' dudes," the driver said. I bumped into Joe's back as he stopped short on the step, surprised by the driver's voice. This man was not the same driver we'd had for the past year and a half. All the other drivers barked orders and were uninterested in us. This guy smiled as we boarded the bus, tipping his cool aviator glasses at the girls like a Southern gentleman while he said, "Mornin' miss."

As seventh graders, we could sit in the middle of the bus, but we took the front seats, curious about this new driver who was speaking to us like we were adults like him.

We learned to not cross the yellow line from the first week of sixth grade. SAISD didn't want students chatting with the drivers and distracting them from driving safely. Eddie's friendliness made us think he might be a rule-breaker, but we didn't want to push it on his first day.

That day, he asked how our Christmas break had been and said, "Have a good day" when we got off the bus at Tafolla. In the months that followed, we continued to sit in the front of the bus. He was always in a good mood, didn't hesitate to curse, and spoke to us like adults, which made me feel so good. It was nice to not get talked down to for once. All the drivers before Eddie were just random adults. I can't even remember what they looked like. Eddie was in his thirties and loved his job; he made being a bus driver cool. I thought being a bus driver can't be that bad of a job because Eddie's doing it, and he's a super-cool guy. He made the bus ride fun. While I'd felt tense on the bus rides for a good part of sixth grade, when Eddie showed up, the bus ride to and from Tafolla was a great way to begin and end the day. Eddie made the bus a safe place to be.

Some days, Eddie would take me, Daniel, and Joe directly home after he dropped the other kids off at Whittier. I didn't know anything about Eddie's job, but we were all pretty sure that this was super against the rules. Man did it feel special to have a thirty-five-foot bus pull up to your front door and drop you off. Eddie would just give us a mischievous smile. I'd go so far to say Eddie was our friend. We loved him because he was nice to us but also because he broke the rules, and we thought that was cool. It was the first time an adult really engaged with us, instead of trying to teach us or control us.

MY FAVORITE TEACHER

By seventh grade I'd only met four black people in my entire life: Tracy, who outran *carrilla* on his birthday; my fifth-grade teacher, Miss Graves; my fourth-grade math teacher, Mr. Mitchell; and my science teacher at Tafolla, Miss Richards. It's funny that three of them were educators, two of them were female, and all four were amazing, impressive people. I also felt really lucky because my mom told me that where she grew up in Laredo, there was one black person in the entire city.

Miss Richards dressed like the black female version of Mister Rogers. She wore flat khakis and a sweater to school every day. The similarities ended there. She had long, curly hair and was thin, scrappy, and rough-looking. She taught middle school science during the school year but more than once talked about her summer research job. She seemed more intelligent, more academic than my other teachers. I'd never met a teacher who worked in her industry during the summer. To me, she was the first person I thought was actually a scientist and because of that, I took everything she said to me very seriously.

She made no apologies for her academic drive. The first day of class she said, "I'm your teacher and I'm hard. I'm going to give you hard assignments, and you're all going to cry and complain. Your parents are going to complain to me on Back to School Night because you've said I'm a jerk. I just want you all to know that every night, I'm going to go home, I'm going to crack open a beer, and I'm going to forget everything you and your parents complained about."

While I could imagine Miss Carter went home and cried after trying to teach Latin all day at Tafolla, it was clear

Miss Richards didn't give a crap about what we or our parents thought about her. That was so punk rock to me, and her tactic worked. We knew she wouldn't put up with any BS, so we didn't dish much out. I grinned during her whole class. She was so smart, and it was awesome to be near that smartness, but I was also respectfully terrified.

One day Miss Richards invited Officer Almendarez, our campus policeman, to speak to our class. He came in with his supervisor, Sergeant Sepulveda, to teach a safety course. I don't know what it had to do with science; maybe it was ordered by the administration or maybe it was her idea as part of keeping control in the classroom. Her street credit grew by having them come to her class. It was real.

Officer Almendarez and Sergeant Sepulveda came in a few times during the year and told real stories about what it's like to be a cop—probably to try to discourage the gang members from committing criminal acts. Sergeant Sepulveda looked and talked like Sylvester Stallone in *Rambo*. So every time he told a story, I would imagine him as Rambo running around San Antonio doing cop stuff. It was so cool in my head. One of the students asked the sergeant if he ever had to pull his gun on someone. He told a story about responding to a call and being tackled by a guy who was trying to get his gun. The sergeant fought off the attacker and arrested him. I could not imagine what kind of moron would try to take a gun from a policeman. Actually, I could imagine one of the guys in SOT being stupid enough to try that.

WRITE IF YOU DARE

Part of Miss Richards's curriculum was writing an essay for Nancy Reagan's DARE campaign against drugs. DARE stood for Drug Abuse Resistance Education, and the tagline was "DARE to say no to drugs." I felt a lot of pressure to write this essay, but I only remember one sentence of it, "The officers in the DARE program are not adults, they're my friends." Not Hemingway, I know, but I tried my best. I won the essay for the whole school and had to read it in the Alamo Stadium in front of three thousand students.

When I won the essay contest, two police officers told me how proud they were of me. I wrote an essay in support of their mission and what they do, and their approval put me in the police officers' camp. I'd never known what it's like to get high until that moment. I wasn't in the police officer gang, per se, but for that moment, I was someone they viewed positively. I knew that if anything happened to me, I would not be lost as some random guy.

It was safe for me to accept the praise and approval of the police officers. Even though I won, I wasn't considered a snitch or a rat or a teacher's pet, because we all had to write an essay about the DARE program and mine happened to be the best one. I also knew if I won, I'd have to read it in public, so if I wrote a brown-nosing and ass-kissing essay, all the students would hear it, and I would have never put myself in that danger.

OFFICER ALMENDAREZ

Officer Almendarez, the school policeman, had a big presence for such a short guy. Everything about him was larger than life—his commanding voice, the way he carried himself. I saw him run for the first time when someone did something in the gymnasium. We couldn't believe how fast he ran, and we students collectively realized we couldn't outrun him, and he gained our instant respect.

He wasn't a security guard from the district. He was part of the San Antonio Police Department, dressed in full police garb, and carried a gun. It was impossible not to feel safe in his presence. He patrolled the whole school alone, all three floors plus the cafeteria, two gyms, and the outside fields. Fights broke out and there were threats between gangs, but for one person, he kept things under control. He was a straight billy badass.

Twice a year the administration would have a "clean your

locker" day. Officer Almendarez brought the drug dogs in the day after. He was so clever that he understood the psychology that after cleaning the lockers, the kids would feel safe to put their drugs, guns, or knives back in their lockers. He and the drug dog busted at least ten kids who had drugs in their lockers. He knew his business.

Officer Almendarez was the guy you wanted in the most violent school in San Antonio. That's what a badass he was. He never talked down to the students nor treated them like children. He asked direct questions and expected direct answers. He offered respect and got respect in return. I never heard a bad word or even a joke about him.

For a while I considered becoming a police officer because of Officer Almendarez. He wasn't tall, nor ripped, or shredded, but he was tough. I wasn't ripped or muscular either, so I thought maybe there was hope for me. I also thought being a police officer meant never being afraid. I was afraid of being hurt most of the time, but no one would hurt him. I thought, "If that's what being a police officer is, sign me up." My mom hated the idea and told me she was going to pray against it, but Officer Almendarez inspired me for a long time. He was a true *toro*, just like me.

MAXIMUM-SECURITY MIDDLE SCHOOL

If Tafolla was the maximum-security middle school, Mr. Alvarado, the principal, and Miss Rodriguez, the vice-principal, were the wardens.

Mr. Alvarado was an academic and very proud of the mission of Tafolla and the multilingual program. He's the one who called Tafolla the Harvard of Middle Schools. He was a big guy, six foot two and 280 pounds, but with a slow walk and kind eyes. Those eyes said that he genuinely cared for all these kids. When you looked at him from the streets, those eyes meant he was weak. I didn't think he had a killer instinct, and unlike Miss Richards or Officer Almendarez, he had neither the street cred nor the fear of the student body.

On the other hand, Miss Rodriguez was terrifying. Her looks were deceiving. She came to school every day in a skirt and high heels, but her piercing eyes were skeptical of everyone and every movement. Her eyes said, "I bet you're up to no good."

She also knew how to use the only weapon she had: her voice. She'd walk down the hall and maim people in the act of misbehaving. When she bellowed, "What are you doing? Get back to class!" Her very voice could throw you up against the lockers.

There was nothing weak about her. She was authoritative and unafraid to dress anyone down for misbehaving. We called her "The Terminator."

While I saw Officer Almendarez everywhere, I feel like I rarely saw Mr. Alvarado or Miss Rodriguez. I felt like the administrators kept to themselves, whereas the teachers and the police officer were a constant presence for the students of Tafolla. They were in our world with us, while the administrators stayed in their realm.

PERMISSION TO ADULT

DEAR LENCH,

In the state of Texas, when you turn sixteen, you are old enough to drive and to get a job. But isn't it weird that in the US, you can join the military at eighteen, go die for your country, but you can't drink alcohol until you're twenty-one? None of it makes any sense and it never will. So what's my point?

My point is that there is no ceremony when you graduate from a young person into being an adult. So consider this letter your Adultness Diploma. Nobody told me this and I wish they had. I didn't feel like an adult until I was thirty-six years old. It has nothing to do with your age and everything to do with your mindset.

Adults evaluate situations and make logical, objective decisions. This is something that you need to start doing. It's so important I'm gonna say it again; adults make decisions for themselves. They take ownership of their feelings, and a healthy adult doesn't try to control the feelings of the people around them.

At this point in your life, you're looking around and evaluating people for behaviors you want to copy, for interests you want to take on—those are adult things. You're looking at your friends and deciding what music, books, movies, even other people you like and don't like. The thing to learn and remember is no one can change your mind. If they change your mind, it's because you changed your mind, not because they forced you to.

The other thing I want you to know is that the adults in your life were doing their best job given what they had. You were skeptical of all adults. You believed they were only there to enforce the rules on you, to make you do homework you didn't want to do, and then they were going to leave you alone in the locker room when bad things would happen.

I need to tell you that that's false.

These adults had great intentions. They were there to protect you, but they couldn't be everywhere at once.

They didn't give you rules and homework to punish you. They were there trying to help you learn things that were important. Some were successful, like Miss Richards, and others weren't, like Miss Carter. Nonetheless, they were trying their best.

As an adult, you have to decide that you are going to take care of yourself even if the other adults around you don't.

In the summer to come, I went to a pre-engineering program called PREP. Part of the program was a math class where we wrote algebraic formulas, which meant having to draw brackets like this: { or }. I had a hard time drawing them, and the teacher called me out. He saw my brackets and said, "No, no, no, no." He walked to the board and copied what I had drawn, saying, "Don't draw like this," and then drew them how they were supposed to be, and said, "Draw like this."

I was completely embarrassed because everybody looked at me as he drew on the board. I went home that day and convinced my mom to let me drop the program, and I never went back.

If a teacher says you have crappy handwriting, an adult has a choice to accept or reject that statement. If you say, "Yes, I have crappy handwriting," then you're on a slippery slope toward saying, "I'm a crappy person." If you choose to say, "I haven't practiced my penmanship enough to be proficient, but today I have decided to practice and get better." The first phrase says, "I surrender and have no control," while the second says, "I'm in charge of what I do and what I can work on to get better." These are totally two different frames of mind.

Do you remember the story of your fourth-grade teacher, Mrs. Reese? That year the class was so bad that I think it broke her. On the last day of school, she walked up and down the row and told each student what was going to happen to them. She said,

"You are going to make it," to one kid.

"You are not going to make it," to another kid.

"You are going to make it," to another.

To the last kid she said, "You. You are going to jail."

I remember that she told Daniel he wasn't going to make it, but she told me that I was going to make it.

Nobody prepares you for some of the self-esteem-crushing words that adults or teachers will say, things like, "You're stupid" or "You're worthless." Your job as an adult is to figure out which of those ideas you allow into your head, and which truth you allow to penetrate your heart.

The hard part, Lench, is that you need to watch these adults and decide whom you're going to learn from and what kind of adult you're going to be. At the same time, the adults around you are speaking things into your life; some of those things are true and some are not true.

In the great bullfight of life, the adult in you is the *matador*. The *toros* are the many words that will charge your mind on a daily basis. You are the only one that can wave the cape and let them pass into your mind. And other times, those words will want to hurt you more than a thousand Spanish bulls. And like a good *matador*, your inner adult needs to draw your sword and kill those words on the spot.

Dramatic I know, but I am who I am. Welcome to adulthood.

CHAPTER 7

BROTHERLY LOVE

As each of us got older and a little bigger, I felt a little safer to be part of the Gomez gang—Danny, Mark, Hector, and me. As the family grew from three to nine, Pops renovated the house to accommodate more kids. By the time there were four boys, my dad enlarged a closet attached to a bedroom so the four of us could sleep in the same space. In the bedroom, there was a three-level bunk bed. I slept on the top, Hector in the middle, and Mark on the bottom trundle that pulled out from underneath the middle bed. Danny slept in the converted closet.

When you're sharing such tight spaces, your personal things become much more important because they're the only things that you feel like you can control. If you feel like you don't have control over even the little things, you freak out. They weren't always fighting, but when they did, it was scary. They fought about stupid things that seem so important when you're a teenager. Mark might have worn Hector's favorite shirt, or Hector borrowed Danny's CDs without telling him.

Looking back, I can see the constant bickering between my brothers just came from teenage angst, but we didn't know how to handle angst or conflict in my family. We would bury it, pretend it didn't bother us, act like nothing had happened, until it would explode into fist fighting.

One of the first times I remember this happening, I was seven years old. I was asleep on the top bunk and woke up because I heard yelling and screaming. I sat up on the top bunk just in time to see my mom burst through the bedroom door in her nightgown and turn on the lights. Danny and Mark were rolling around on Danny's bed. One of them had the other pinned, and to the right of them, there was a huge hole in the wall. One of them had put the other's head through the sheetrock.

As soon as I saw the scene, I started crying. My mom pointed to me and said, "Look, you're scaring Lencho." Instantly Danny and Mark stopped fighting. In that moment I consciously realized I had some control over my brothers' behavior.

I was a lot younger than the three of them. The summer of 1994, I was fourteen, Danny was twenty-four, Mark was twenty, and Hector was nineteen. Among the three of them, there was a lot of testosterone in those tight sleeping quarters. All three of them played football, and their notion of fighting was physical. They would yell, but that wasn't enough—they went straight for the tackle.

My brothers' anger was explosive, and I was afraid of getting caught in the middle of their fights. They were in the prime of their physical fitness and worked out regularly. I was petrified when they fought because they were bigger and stronger than me, and with one misfire I would have been a dead *toro*.

We were standing in the kitchen the night Hector accused Mark of lending a favorite Depeche Mode CD to one of his friends. Like the gang fights at Tafolla, fights between my brothers went down fast but I could see it coming as their voices started to get louder. They both took a step back. They squared up, puffing their chests and curling their hands into tight fists. I ran between them, putting a hand on each of their chests, and said, "Don't fight." They tried to push me away as they walked toward each other. I refused to be pushed aside and fought my way to stay in between them. When they realized they couldn't throw down without accidentally hitting me, they backed down.

Mom walked in and said, as she often did, "Lencho is my little peacemaker. You're so brave."

I was a nervous wreck. I worried about school, I worried about getting shot at the corner store, and then if things escalate at home because someone's wearing someone else's favorite T-shirt, I've got to be on alert to make sure it doesn't go down in my own room.

REVENGE FOR HECTOR

Hector had the same body frame that I did, which meant we were lean in our teens and filled out as adults. But unlike me, he was fearless. In football, he would always try to tackle the guy who was twice his size. He would sacrifice his entire body if he had to, and it left an impression on everyone. He was especially fun to watch because bigger players would pay no attention to Hector, which is what he wanted. Next thing you know, Hector would come out of nowhere full speed and lay your ass out. You knew it hurt him; he just didn't care. My brother Mark was a genetic mutant in the best way in my family. He was stronger, he could run faster, and he was physically superior to all the other Gomezes in every other way—oh, and was more of a ladies man. Hector would fight five guys knowing at least one of them would regret it the next day. Mark would fight five guys and make them wish they were never born.

When Hector and Mark were in high school at Thomas Edison, there was a guy named Robert who was just nothing but trouble. The word on the street was that he had beef with my brother Mark. I didn't know anything about this guy, but I did know one thing. There was a 1,000 percent chance that whoever he was, he wasn't good enough to take my brother Mark in a fight. I'd bet my money on that.

He probably knew that, too, which is probably why he decided to take a coward's strategy. He wanted to hurt Mark and decided the way to do it was through our family. He waited one day for my brother Hector to go to the showers after football practice. While my brother was in the shower, defenseless, with soap in his eyes, this piece of shit jumped him. Robert was fully dressed and wearing steel-toe Red Wing boots.

All I saw was the aftermath.

I had never felt that much hate and rage in my entire life. I'd never seen my parents so angry. It was one of the only times in my life where the entire Gomez family was unified by one intense feeling of anger and injustice. The anger hung in the air. I had never seen what steel-toe boots could do to a person. I couldn't bring myself to look at Hector, and when I finally did all I could do was cry. I'd never seen someone close to me who'd been jumped.

Anger at the injustice of the fight swelled inside of me, too. I knew if Hector had been dressed, if the odds had been fair, Hector would have wiped the floor with him. I also noticed something abnormal for my peaceful, compassionate, Jesus-loving, turn-the-other-cheek parents. They were trying to calm us down, especially Mark because they knew what he was going to do. But inside I could tell they were conflicted. I could tell they wanted revenge for their son, but they couldn't say so. In the end they told Mark he wasn't allowed to go after Robert. But Mark's eyes were like the *toro* whose eyes said he would charge the very gates of Hell to get revenge.

The next day, my parents called the school because they wanted to warn the principal that Mark was probably going to try to find Robert. By the time they called it was too late. Mark saw Robert and beat his ass right outside the principal's office. He came home suspended, and my parents said they were upset, but their body language told a different story. There was no yelling or reproach because justice had been rendered for Hector.

Two years later, we heard that Robert had committed suicide. That day there was no sympathy from the Gomez family. Our silence paid him no regard.

HONEYCOMBS AND SHOTGUN SHELLS

Felix, Roseanna, and their three children, Beth, Tammy, and Tony, lived across the street but their family was nothing like mine. One day the youngest daughter, Tammy, told my mom that we were rich. Mom asked her why she thought that, she said, "Because you have ice trays. Only rich people have ice trays in their freezer." We had five ice trays—we must have been millionaires.

Beth came crying to my mom one day complaining that Roseanna told her to clean the whole house. Mom said, "Why are you crying? Why can't you just clean it?" Beth said, "Mrs. Gomez, there's so many beer bottles. Everybody just pees on the wall and I have to clean it up."

Their son Tony stuttered. The rumor was he got that stutter because Roseanna would put a knife in his hand when Felix was asleep and say, "You need to kill Felix, because you're a kid and they won't send you to jail."

One day I was hanging out with my friends at the house next to Felix and Roseanna's house. Felix and Roseanna were fighting, and we saw Roseanna take a hammer to their windows while she screamed. I watched the glass fly away from the house as she smashed one after another from the inside.

That was the kind of family that lived across the street.

In my house, we made jokes about how rich we were with our ice trays. We also ate cereal before we went to bed. Pops had a sweet tooth, and every night around ten o'clock he'd get a hankering for a slice of cake or a bowl of ice cream. We followed his example, and every night my siblings and I would eat a few handfuls of sugary cereal. We each had a favorite. Mine and Hector's favorite cereal was Honeycombs.

A typical summer evening at ten, Hector and I were eating Honeycombs when we heard the loudest gunshot we'd ever heard. Somehow, I knew it was from a shotgun— maybe from watching too many movies—but I knew.

No sooner had the gunshot echo faded, the flashing red and blue lights of the cop cars reflected in our windows as they pulled up to the house across the street. We went outside to our front yard and Beth and Tammy came running to my mom.

Mom asked what had happened. Tammy said sobbing, "Mrs. Gomez! My dad shot my mom because she was wearing his pants." We were so confused by this, but Beth later explained that the real argument had been about who wore the pants in the family, and in his rage, Felix took out a shotgun and blew off Roseanna's calf.

The next day, I went to visit Tony, and there was a huge

puddle of blood on their front porch. Before thinking, I said, "Wow. Your mom has a lot of blood."

My mom went to visit Roseanna in the hospital, ministering to those in need as she often did. She said Roseanna needed Jesus in her heart. Roseanna said, "Mrs. Gomez, when I was a little kid my parents owned a bar. At the end of the bar there was a fruit bowl but instead of fruit, the bowl was full of heroin. Anybody who came into the bar could help themselves to heroin. That's all I know, Mrs. Gomez."

Felix went to jail for a few months. When he got out, they got back together just like any other dysfunctional couple would do.

It was only the street that separated our two houses. But our houses could have been two different countries separated by the ocean. That is how different things were on West Hermosa Street.

MUSIC

As we all got older, we added on to our little house again because there was no way to keep the peace anymore with four boys in one bedroom. My brothers and I helped Pops do the construction work. The house kept getting longer, and we used to joke that one day it would hit the highway. Danny, being the oldest, got one of the bigger bedrooms. I'd hang out there a lot and he didn't seem to mind. Even though there are ten years between us, I've always been closest to him.

Danny loved music, and one of the first things he bought when he started having disposable income was a stereo system with a receiver and big speakers. I thought he had to be a millionaire to afford that stereo. I remember the scene many years later in *Almost Famous* where the guy's older sister gives him all her records. Danny was just like that. I'd be in Danny's room playing with toys or reading comic books, while Danny listened to *Just Like Heaven* by The Cure or New Order's *Substance* album. Even though I was a little kid, I knew all the songs and began to have favorites. He'd make suggestions for other music based on what I liked.

Because of his love of music, Danny loved going to concerts, and he'd take as many of us with him as he could afford. My sister Sonia loved Blondie and 10,000 Maniacs. Hector liked Rage Against the Machine, but I suspect it was for the mosh pit to let out his teenage angst. Danny took any sibling who was interested in music to concerts.

Mom and Pops gave Danny more leeway than the rest of us. He didn't go out of his way to get into trouble and was always very chill. He wanted to listen to music. He was a hard worker and was going to school to be an x-ray technician just like my dad had done. He was a reader. My parents trusted him and let me go to my first concert with him. We came home super happy and no one got beat up, so they let me go again.

Given how important faith was to Mom and Pops, you'd think they would have outlawed grunge and punk rock in the house, but music was important to them. Growing up, we all remember dancing in the kitchen with Mom to Sam Cooke. Pops loved the Mexican band Los Dandys; we listened to the same cassette on our car trips to Laredo and he would sing to Mom along with the love songs. I think they loved music so much they didn't want to take it away from us.

The first concert he took me to was Cheap Trick and Stray Cats at the Tower of the Americas in downtown San Antonio. I was probably nine years old. A group of tough bikers stood in front of us and they were impressed that a little kid knew all the Stray Cats songs, so they made space for me to see the stage. When the Stray Cats played a cover of *I Fought the Law*, everyone lost their minds. Then, when Cheap Trick came out everyone was waiting for their famous song, *I Want You to Want Me*, but my favorite song was *Surrender*. When they played it, I was convinced they'd played it just for me. I felt as tall as those bikers.

I remember the day I first heard and saw the video for Nirvana's *Smells like Teen Spirit*—back when MTV played music. The hair rose on my arms when the video came on. I knew I was watching something new that was not from this world. So I thought life couldn't get any cooler when Danny told me that he had gotten us tickets to the upcoming Lollapalooza where Nirvana was going to play. If you had offered me a trip to the White House to meet the President, I would have turned it down to see Nirvana.

In April of 1994, we went to a Breeders concert at a place called The Showcase in San Antonio. That year I feel like we were on a roll going to see so many cool bands as they came through San Antonio. But The Breeders was special because it was the first band I ever loved where the core of the band was women. Kim and Kelly Deal were the first rock stars I ever had crushes on. That day I was so excited to see them, and the opening band had finished playing and we were waiting for The Breeders to start. Then, a guy walked up to the mic and announced that Kurt Cobain had committed suicide. The whole club lost it. We didn't know what to do and it almost ruined the night. It wasn't until The Breeders took the stage and dedicated their first song, *Driving on 9*, to him that we were able to enjoy the concert. Nirvana had such an influence on me, as did The Red Hot Chili Peppers, Stone Temple Pilots, and Pearl Jam, who were all new around that same time frame. This was the first time I saw a group of outsiders who looked different than other people, and that's how I felt. And, they were getting famous and making great music. I loved all the grunge music that influenced the flannel shirts the KFCs wore. If they'd gone to Tafolla, we would have been friends.

I was dedicated to the whole persona of a grunge or punk rocker. My brother bought me a T-shirt at every concert, but I was small, so the shirts were always too big, and it looked weird. I wore them anyway. I practically slept in my Pearl Jam T-shirt all through seventh and eighth grade. I wore combat boots that were two sizes too big because they didn't come in my size. I was very snobbish about it—Doc Martens were for posers, well, except for Ivan who could pull it off. Combat boots were what real people wore. I shaved my head because I saw punk rockers with shaved heads and mohawks.

Danny took me to Dallas to go to another Lollapalooza at the Starplex Amphitheater. We drove there and spent the night in a hotel. We ordered in pizza and ate in our hotel room. He also brought Hector, Sonia, and our cousin Judy with us because she liked the same kind of music. I was loving life, enjoying music and a pizza in a hotel room with my family. This was the first time I ever got a real sense of what it felt like to take a vacation. I loved it.

One of the bands at Lollapalooza that year was Shonen Knife from Japan. The band was three Japanese girls who spoke almost no English. We were all very proud because Danny had found them from some obscure magazine that he got every month on new bands. Danny loved finding new bands. We felt so cool when we saw that Shonen Knife was playing, because most people didn't know who they were, but we did. Their songs were happy, and we were giddy, dancing in the rain, singing along, and watching them sing their song *Riding on the Rocket*, on one of the side stages.

After the summer, I went back to Tafolla and shared all the new music I knew with Martin, Ivan, Big Mac, and Joe, who all loved the same bands I did. We bonded over music, and it became part of my identity. In school, the Kool Flannel Club was our way of expressing ourselves. Music became more important than ever.

CREATING SAFETY VS. CONTROLLING OTHERS

DEAR LENCH,

Do you remember how often Mom called you the little peacemaker? She would say, "Lencho's my little peacemaker, and he's not afraid to get in front of his brothers and stop them from fighting." Well, many years later I went to therapy and I had a breakthrough about this story.

It has to do with feeling safe. In short, the reason you were prepared to sacrifice your body was not because you were brave, or you were a peacemaker. You were afraid.

Each time they were going to fight, a part of your brain craved safety and started doing the math on how to achieve it. First, your brain figured out that Mom and Pops couldn't control them because they were bigger and stronger. Then, it figured out that they weren't going to rationally talk this out. Once your brain saw new violence was coming, your body said, "If I throw myself in between them, they won't risk hurting me."

Your fear of their fighting was greater than your fear of being hurt. And in that fear, you created safety in a very unhealthy way. You manipulated the behavior of your brothers. Sure, you did it for a good reason but that does not matter.

That behavior was not healthy.

It's not healthy, because you were controlling the behavior of others, and that is a problem. One of the things that you need to know is that if you do something or don't do something, or if you say something or don't say something, to control the behavior of someone else—that is an unhealthy behavior in human relationships. If you use guilt, shame, or manipulation to control other people's feelings, that is not healthy. And, if someone does something or doesn't do something to control how you behave, that's also not healthy.

A great example of someone at church saying, "The Lord doesn't approve of that." It very well might be true, but the intent is key. If they are trying to control your behavior, then they are using guilt to do it.

When you try to control others—or they try to control you—you're saying, "I know what's best for you." Danny, instead, took a healthier approach, which is, "Let me create a safe place for you to listen to all this music, and you decide what you like and what you don't like."

Part of the job of the adult is to create a safe place for you to explore things like music and decide for yourself. Danny wasn't saying, "I'd love you more if you love Nirvana or if you loved New Order." He was saying, "Oh, my God. You're into music, let me just show you this buffet of stuff. And it's okay to listen to it here in my room with headphones on. No one will judge you if you like that song. You get to pick."

One of the things no one tells you that you need to learn growing up is we have to create a safe place for each other and for ourselves to discover new things without being manipulated by others and the preference of others.

You tried to manipulate your brothers to create a safe place for yourself, but there are ways to create safety without manipulation and control.

We need to stop and say that this is one of those things that you see everywhere, and no one has ever called it out. I'm calling it out because you have to pay attention to it if you ever want to be a healthy adult.

Awareness is step one. The second thing, and the only thing that you can and should do, is stop and take ownership of what you're feeling and what your actions are. This is the hardest part. You have to adopt healthy talk. Healthy talk says, "I am feeling very discouraged right now and I would really love a hug from you." Own your feelings and ask for what you need and want.

You have to own that the only thing you control is you. How does controlling what you do play out in these situations? It looks like this, "I'm scared that someone at school is going to beat me up," which is owning that you are afraid. Now, your action is what you do. You say, "I have decided to tell my parents, a teacher, or some other adult who I think can help me feel safe." You're still owning, but now you are also taking action.

Some of this may sound silly or corny, but I am here to tell you that it is not. This is Jedi, black-belt level of adulting.

And take it from me, when you do it right, you will get the best sleep you have ever had in your life.

CHAPTER 8

~~~~~~~~~~

SANDBAG SHOWDOWN

Abel was a regular from the Westside and one of the members of the SOT. This was weird because most of the SOT were multilingual students. But as time passed, there was a small but growing number of regulars who joined. He stood out because he was handsome—not something you can say about most eighth-graders. Early in September I walked into homeroom and all the girls were crying, so I knew something bad had happened. In between their sobs, I was able to piece together what had happened. Abel was at a payphone in the Courts, when some guy walked up behind him and shot him in the back of the neck. The bullet exited his cheek, and he lived.

The Studs of Tafolla were increasingly picking fights with students, especially with us, the KFC. If we hadn't formed a gang, they probably wouldn't have even noticed us, but once we declared ourselves a gang with a name, we were the enemy. My first thought when I heard Abel was shot was, "Good," and I wished that he had died. I was conflicted because I knew I shouldn't want anyone to get shot, but I really hated how scared the SOT made me feel, and I was bummed the shooter didn't finish the job. I was just so tired of being afraid all the time.

Eighth grade began in 1995, and the gang tension was high. Every day my fight response got a little stronger than my flight response. I'd never been touched by anyone in or out of Tafolla, but the threat of being jumped was so intense, I began to consider doing things I wasn't normally willing to do.

"STEP ON THAT ROACH"

The KFC just wanted to be left alone, talk about music, comic books, and Quentin Tarantino movies, and occasionally play basketball. Every once in while, we would play basketball with the regulars and the other gangs.

We had no choice because most days, despite begging whichever teacher was playground monitor that day, we were given only one basketball, rarely two. If we were lucky enough to have two basketballs, one group could play full court and one group could play half court. Most days, five gangs competed for one basketball. The KFC was always outnumbered by the other gangs. Most of the time, we wouldn't bother trying to get the ball and would simply go to a corner along the back fence of the court that we'd chosen as our territory.

Boy did we want to play basketball, though.

It was a complete accident, but we happened to have some of the best basketball players in the school in KFC. Big Mac was by far the tallest guy on the court and our other friend Kevin was amazing. After months and months of begging, there was one semester in seventh grade when my parents agreed to let me play on the official Tafolla Basketball team. I didn't make the A team, but I was a B team starter, which was awesome. The problem was, we sucked. I am not 100 percent positive, but I'm pretty sure that we lost every single game that year. Every single game. Losing, however, never took the fun out of lunchtime basketball.

We got in a game one day with the regulars, hardcore Westside guys against us, the punk rockers. At one point I got the ball. I was tiny and skinny, but I was fast. I dribbled the ball and ran, in and out of the arms and legs of the regulars team. Nobody could catch me. Valentino, a tall, light-skinned Mexican with a Marine-style buzz cut was trying to block me. He was a good basketball player, but you never knew what you'd get with Val; some days he was a jerk and other days he was nice. Today it didn't matter because he was no match for my speed. I zipped by Val, and in his frustration, he yelled, "Somebody, step on that roach!" And just like that; the game stopped. People were rolling around on the court laughing, and the game was over. I still had the ball and had no idea what to do, so I just stood there. His timing was so perfect and frustration so real that no one could let it go. From that instant and for the rest of my time at Tafolla, my new nickname was Roach.

Not everyone was on the basketball court, but my new name spread like wildfire throughout the student body. I was in the locker room a couple days later and the twins stopped in front of me. They were kind of cool because they were twins and they were good basketball players, but they were also hard-core fighters and drug addicts from the Westside, so I was afraid of them. They said, "Hey, are you Roach?" I hesitantly said, "Yeah, man." Their eyes widened, they smiled and nodded, rocking a little bit, "Oh, dude. That's so cool, man. Do you have any roaches?" I instantly relaxed when I realized that they were talking about marijuana. They thought I'd been given the nickname Roach because I was a pothead. I never confessed that I had never even seen weed, much less smoked it. In fact, I didn't know what a roach was, but I knew it was a thing because my neighbors talked about it. The twins didn't need to know that.

My whole outlook on my new nickname changed. I hated when Val first called me Roach, but now I realized it could be used to make friends. All of a sudden, I had been rebranded; I was Lorenzo Roach, the pothead. I went with it and chuckled to myself thinking, "I have to ride this train."

My nickname gave me confidence. It gave strangers a way to talk to me and a way for me to talk to strangers, which I did not have before. Before Roach, I was an anonymous, tiny brown guy in a sea of tiny brown guys, but with the name Roach, I stood out. Now there was something special about me, a common way for people to get to know me. People who would have never come up and talked to me now did so because I had a name that made them think they knew something about me, something that maybe we had in common.

To this day, I hold Val with disdain in my heart because I know he called me a cockroach. If my brand had been Lorenzo the Cockroach, I would have been an, angry, bitter eighth-grader. The twins came along and innocently re-branded my name to something dangerous and cool. How many people out there have a name that's the former, not the latter? To me, I was very lucky to get re-branded, but if they hadn't, I probably wouldn't even tell you the story.

WHAT'S IN A (GANG) NAME?

Around that same time Danny and I started going to a Southern Baptist mega-church, where the pastor was an amazing storyteller. He held my short attention like no other pastor. He acted out the stories he told, yelling and screaming in parts, and I was captivated. Shortly after I was baptized "Roach," the pastor preached a fire and brimstone sermon about the name of Jesus. He said, "Shakespeare writes, 'What's in a name? If a rose were called by any other name, would it smell just as sweet?' Shakespeare had it wrong. There is power in a name."

His words stuck in my head. The name does matter. As soon as we called ourselves the KFC, our name said to the other gangs, "We're in the game, now, and we just admitted that we're in the game." We didn't know that, and it was a foolish mistake on our part. We were doing it to mock the other gangs, but the flip-side of our joke is that it sent a message to everybody that said, "We're here to be in the game that is gang culture." Our name made us a unified target.

IT'S NOT SAFE HERE

One day a big guy named Edward saved my neck when he didn't have to. I was walking past Miss Richards's science class and Edward was standing in the hall like he was waiting for something. He saw me and got a worried look. He walked up to me and said, "Hey, Roach, it's not safe here. It's about to go down." He picked me up by the shoulders and moved me from the center of the hallway to the wall near some lockers.

Two seconds later a ten-person brawl erupted, and Edward was in the middle of it. The fight went down just outside Miss Richards's room. True to form, she came running out of her room, throwing guys around to break up the fight. She was absolutely fearless and was a sight to behold—a female African-American teacher breaking up a Mexican gang fight. I was petrified, frozen in my safe zone between the lockers watching Miss Richards separate these *vatos* like she was trained by the San Antonio Police Department. The whole scene reminded me of the song *Come Out and Play* by The Offspring. I'd have to remember to listen to that later on the bus ride.

Truth is, I knew before it went down that something was up. I'd gotten so used to seeing fights that I knew what to look for. An eerie silence hung in the air before a fight and the fighters' body language was tense. They'd clench their teeth and stand a little straighter, their bodies stiff, waiting for the attack.

I remember one of my brothers giving me advice on what to do if I was in that same situation. He said, "If you know it's going to go down, don't wait for them to throw the first punch. If you know it's going down, you punch them first and you punch them fast. And if their friend is there, you punch him too, and if their girlfriend is there, you punch her too. And if their mom is there, you punch her too, you punch everyone."

But I didn't want to punch anyone. That's not who I was. I just wanted to put on my headphones and listen to *Interstate Love Song* by Stone Temple Pilots.

The tension made me so afraid. The almost-fights were more frightening than the actual fights, because once a fight was over, the tension eased. If a fight almost happened, but didn't, the tension continued to build. I didn't know when or how it would happen, so I lived with the feeling that I had to constantly watch my back.

SANDBAGS BEGIN TO FLY

The walls around the basketball court were almost always covered with graffiti. The funny thing is, I never saw anyone actually do the graffiti, which means people were coming into the schoolyard at night or the weekends. The school district would hire a company to sandblast the walls a couple times a year and then bleach them. They'd stay clean for a few days and then the graffiti artists went back to work. Good sized hills of sand collected around the basketball court, and of course the gangs found a way to turn sand into something bad. Every other lunchtime, they would take empty potato chip bags and plastic soda bottles and fill them with sand.

One day, I was minding my own business, playing 21 with the rest of the KFC crew on the half-court at lunch. Then out of nowhere, a Doritos bag full of sand crashed on the court, almost hitting us. We turned and saw the guys in the SOT laughing and pointing. One guy was ready to launch the second bag.

Ivan turned and said, "What the hell, dude?" to the SOT, and started walking in their direction. We stopped him. We were outnumbered and didn't really know what to do.

It was clear they wanted to provoke us into a fight. It was also clear that the last thing we wanted was a fight—most of us at least. Over the next couple of weeks they kept throwing sandbags trying to instigate a fight, waiting for us to do anything that would justify their full-on attack—stare at them, talk trash to them, or throw something back. All the other gangs were watching to see what would go down. There was enough space between us that we walked away and sat down in the corner, trying to get out of the line of fire. They threw sandbags at us for what seemed like the whole lunch period.

The KFC crew was split on how to respond. Half of us

were happy to keep dodging bags of sand for the rest of the year, and the other half wanted to fight and not let them disrespect us. Throwing sandbags at us became a regular occurrence.

Until somebody got fed up. We were playing full-court basketball and a bag of sand and glass landed on the court. Somebody from KFC said, "What the hell, asshole!" The game came to a standstill. Everybody stopped and squared up. About ten SOTs walked over and tried to stare us down. Like two packs of dogs sniffing each other without touching. One of their biggest tried to get in Big Mac's face. This guy tried to get nose to nose with Big Mac, but he wasn't tall enough.

He looked up at Big Mac, talking trash, "You guys think you're all badass or what...fuck KFC." Big Mac stood still staring down at him in silence.

There are moments in my life when all of a sudden everything is crystal clear. I was standing—all seventy pounds of me—in fear, and I saw this guy was talking trash because he was nervous. He was trying to project how tough he was, but he was a scared sissy inside. Big Mac's silence scared him. Big Mac's stare said it all. It said, "Step up, dude. I will eat your soul." This punk knew the score and finally backed off.

I knew that tension before a fight all too well. I'd seen

it plenty of times with my brothers, but I could calm my brothers. There was nothing I could do to calm this tension. Nothing went down—that day—but I started thinking I needed to put an end to these guys.

We had a win on our side because they didn't have the guts to fight Big Mac, but the verbal abuse kept going up. The sandbags kept raining down. I don't know what we did to them, but they wanted to fight us badly.

MAKING A PLAN

A week later, I was walking toward the basketball court at lunchtime and saw Raymond, the Junior Mexican Mafia leader. He said, "What's up, Roach, how's it going, man?" I said, "I'm good, man, what's up with you?" and walked over to talk to him. "Hey, man, don't you think the Studs of Tafolla are kind of assholes?" I asked. He said, "Yeah, dude, I hate those guys." I said, "I have been thinking: What if we all just jumped them?"

"Yeah," he said, "I'd be down with that, Roach." Raymond's second in command, the silent chubby Mexican kid standing next to him, nodded in agreement. "Let us know, *vato*."

For the first time in my entire life, I was slowly starting to look forward to a fight. My family always loved watching

The Godfather and it was one of the few movies my dad loved quoting. Suddenly I felt like I was calling a meeting with the heads of the five families. Only it wasn't to call a truce, it was to declare war.

A plan began to take shape. I felt more confident because Raymond was down with my plan. Now I daydreamed of broken noses and black eyes.

I knew I could sell the idea to Big Mac, Ivan, and the rest of the guys if I could build a big enough posse. I had the first chess piece with Raymond's crew on board. If I could get the NDs on our side, that would be game over. The ND crew were the biggest, baddest, strongest *vatos* in our school. They were chill and not all that violent, as if they were above middle school shenanigans. One in particular, though, Adrian, loved that my name was Roach; I knew I could sell him on the idea. It was amazing how much currency I got off of my nickname.

I worked on this plan in my head and didn't tell a single soul, but I was still only fourteen years old. All I knew was that KFC, Raymond's Crew, and the NDs were enough to stomp those little bitches into eternity. And then I'd make those *putos* choke on those bags of sand.

The tension continued to rise, and I hadn't talked to Adrian yet. One day in November I couldn't stand it anymore and decided that day was the day. I'd go to the ND part of the basketball court after lunchtime, in full view of everyone, and talk to Adrian. When people saw me climb up the steps to go talk to them, they'd be asking themselves, "What's Roach doing, going to the ND territory?" but once he agreed to fight the SOT, it wouldn't matter.

I sat in our spot at the back of the basketball court, waiting for Adrian to show up. I was so nervous that all I could do was play Pantera's song *Mouth for War* on my Walkman to build up my courage. I was humming nervously when out of nowhere, I heard a burst of a commotion. I looked up and Adrian was running and laughing, the rest of his crew running behind him. I heard someone say, "Hey, it's Adrian's birthday today." The law of *carrilla* was about to be dished out. Adrian ran into the bathroom, followed by his crew and the entire SOT gang not wanting to miss a single punch.

BUSTED

During this time, I wasn't the only one who felt the tension at Tafolla. Officer Almendarez had noticed it too. As the SOTs followed Adrian into the bathroom, police officers emerged from everywhere. We'd been so self-involved we'd never noticed the cops on the roof around the school who had been watching us. Officer Almendarez and the San Antonio Police Department had led a mini-sting operation on our students.

The day that this *carrilla* went down on Adrian was the day the cops made their move. The bathroom where Adrian was about to get jumped was just the epicenter. A huge commotion took over the entire school. There were dozens of students—fourteen-year-olds in middle school—in handcuffs face down on the floor.

We wisely stayed on our corner of the basketball court until the chaos settled down. I don't think we were on anyone's radar. We walked back toward the school and saw the aftermath of the throw down. I walked out the front door and saw two police vans full of Studs of Tafolla and NDs that the cops had been watching. That day, the school district expelled them from Tafolla and sent them all to different schools.

I didn't have to finish my grand master plan of jumping the SOT. I probably couldn't have pulled it off if I wanted to, and I'm glad I didn't have to find out. So much of my anxiety went away knowing that the sandbag throwing would stop, I wouldn't have to fight, and the tension would end.

ANGER AND FEAR—REVENGE AND JUSTICE

DEAR LENCH,

First, I want to tell you about the power of a name. And just like a Southern Baptist preacher once said, "There is power in a name. A name that you tell yourself can be rocket fuel or deadly poison. A name has the power to lift you up high and the power to drown you in a sea of depression."

You could have told yourself the name Roach meant you were an ugly insect that everybody hates and wants to step on, that you're no good or a pest. Instead, you told yourself you were kind of dangerous. A lot of times in life, people will give you names that you need to fight. Some of them look like, "You're Stupid. You're Ugly. You're unloved." Those labels are the same as being called Roach or Princess. Someone can murder your self-esteem with a name or raise your self-esteem from the dead.

In your case, you did a great job of reminding yourself what is true, which is, "I am not this insect to be stepped on. I am a human being who is worthy of dignity and respect."

When you run into the parts of your life where someone gives you a name that poisons your mind, it is your job to tell yourself that it's not true. You'll see it happen to other people, too. It is also your job as a human to tell other people that their name is not true about them. I say this because in life it's easy to fall into the game where we make fun of people and we think everyone is having a good time. But if you are giving someone a name, just remember that words have power. And if the name you are giving someone does not build them up, then you need to stop, apologize, and do everything in your power to lift them up with your words. If not, you will go down in history as their Valentino. Resist at all costs.

ANGER AND FEAR

I've already mentioned one of my favorite mentors, author and pastor Dr. Tim Keller. He once said, "Anger is the dynamite of the soul." I love how he puts it in perspective. In the same way dynamite is not a bad thing, neither is anger. But it is dangerous and just like dynamite, you have to handle it with care and respect.

Despite what anyone tells you, it is not a bad thing to get angry. As the good book says, our goal is "to be slow to anger." In life, when you see the people and things you love threatened, it should absolutely make you angry. And if you don't ever get angry that means you don't love anything and that is bad. The problem is that most people don't know how to control their anger, and so they are unstable sticks of dynamite walking around and destroying everything in their path.

For me, I have found that if I can just create some time and space between my anger and my action, I can normally control it. That means writing the angry text or email but not sending it. Maybe even sleeping on it. It means making yourself go for a walk or a drive before you explode. It means telling yourself to not say what you want to say in the heat of the moment. If you can even put seconds between you and your anger, you will normally make far better decisions.

When you were fourteen, you thought you were angry, but I want to tell you that underneath that anger was fear. You thought you were angry at the Studs of Tafolla, but you were afraid. I am sorry that you were so afraid that you had to entertain revenge. I am sorry that you were even in that position. No one tells you that when you are really afraid, you are willing to do things that are abnormal, that are outside of your character.

You thought you were so angry that you had had enough and that you were going to inflict the same fear they had inflicted on you. You wanted to get revenge. You wanted them put in their place. You wanted them to feel what you were feeling. You wanted them to stop, but I'm here to tell you that if you had executed that plan, nothing would have changed. It wouldn't have stopped them. They wouldn't have respected you. All you would have done is light the dynamite and made everything worse.

REVENGE AND JUSTICE

So often we tell ourselves that revenge is giving someone what they deserve. This is one of the greatest lies of them all. Revenge is like a drug addiction because it creates a cycle that you think you are in control of when in fact it controls you.

Let's just pretend that you got everybody together, and you absolutely destroyed the SOTs. I'm telling you right now, it would not have fixed anything. First, do you think any of those guys would have taken an ass beating and not planned on getting back at you? That is exactly what they would have done, and the cycle would have just begun. Second, you would have immediately felt guilt and shame about your part in it. Even if you gave the last kick in the face to the Studs of Tafolla, you would take the burden of the guilt and shame with you for the rest of your life. It's the kind of guilt and shame that keeps you up at night. But they don't tell that part in movies.

Revenge is out in the world, and you need to stay far away from it because revenge is a poison. If you think you can control the poison, you are sadly mistaken. It will poison you, and it will destroy you from the inside out.

What you experienced at the end of the SOT story was justice.

You can't underestimate adults. It looks like they're not paying attention, and you think you're smarter than they are, but they know who the troublemakers are. You had written them off. You chose not to engage them. You chose not to call for help. You decided to take matters into your own hands, yet all the time there they were, standing, watching, planning, and using their resources to create safety.

They saw the tension rising just like you did, and they, too, made a plan—of justice not revenge—to do something about it. They wanted peace and safety for you and all the students. They were waiting for the right moment for their sting operation to have the greatest impact.

In the end, their plan brought justice, peace, and order back to Tafolla. You need to acknowledge they did the right thing. I am thankful that they were doing what adults should do, which is looking out for the students and creating a safe place for you. And when you lose hope and think justice is never served, remember the day the adults swooped in and brought safety back to Tafolla. Life is not always fair, but I am happy to say, it was fair that day.

Now, stretch your legs, play some basketball, and see what it feels like to shoot hoops without having to worry.

CHAPTER 9

~~~~~~

LAST DAY OF MIDDLE SCHOOL

AND ON TO HIGH SCHOOL

The Kool Flannel Club had no idea how much the undercover police raid would set us free to be ourselves. It was as if overnight we replaced worry with hope and excitement. And as we felt freer to be ourselves, we started to get creative. We had been bottling up who we really were and now we boldly started to come out of our shells.

We all loved Quentin Tarantino's *Reservoir Dogs*. I don't remember who thought of it. Maybe Daniel or Big Mac said, "Hey, we should all dress up as Reservoir Dogs on the last day of school." We were a bunch of poor kids who couldn't afford black suits, so we showed up wearing black pants, white button-up shirts, black ties, and shades.

The greatest thing was that we all did it. A dozen of us dressed like Reservoir Dogs and we were the talk of the last day of school. We ended our last day at Tafolla on such a high because we knew we weren't going to get our asses kicked, and we were, for the first time in three years, able to show our personalities and who we were. We weren't just KFC anymore. We were these kids who loved movies, music, video games, and comic books. We got to express ourselves on the very last day of school. And just like Andy Dufresne in *The Shawshank Redemption*, we crawled through a river of shit and came out Reservoir Dogs on the other side.

HEALTH CAREERS

The high of the last day of school was followed by a sobering thought. I was losing my friends from Tafolla.

The regular students from Tafolla had no choice but to go to Lanier, which, if you can imagine, was ten times worse than Tafolla. Someone told me once that a student bombed a teacher's car, but I could never figure out if it was true. That was the Lanier reputation. At least Tafolla had a cool mascot like the *Toro*. Lanier's mascot was a Volk. What the hell was a Volk anyway? I asked a teacher out of curiosity and she told me that the Volk was short for vocational, which is what the school was designed for. Lanier was built to give these students vocational skills like welding and working on cars, so they could get a job. The message was the high school expected no one to go to college. I thought to myself, "Man, that's fucked up."

The multilingual students had more options. I could go to my neighborhood high school, Thomas Edison High School, or Brackenridge High School, which was the continuation of the multilingual program. My four older siblings had gone to Edison, and my parents said there was no way I was going to Edison. Most of the multilingual students were going to Brackenridge High School, which to me was way better than going to Edison.

There was a third option. Pops was an x-ray technician his whole career and some of the doctors talked about an amazing school called Health Careers. It was ranked the number one high school in San Antonio, and because it was a charter school, it accepted students outside of the ZIP code and was free to attend. My older sister Sonia was in her last year of the Health Careers when I was a freshman, and Mom and Pops thought it would be a good school for me, too.

Unfortunately for me, you had to have almost straight A's to get accepted—I should have paid more attention in Latin class. I had flunked a couple of classes in eighth grade, so I wasn't eligible for Health Careers. My parents have never been so upset with me. I was disappointed, but at least I would know people at Brackenridge. I wouldn't be alone.

BRACKENRIDGE

Come late August, I had recovered from the anxiety of Tafolla and was ready to attend Brackenridge High School.

On the first day of school, I started to realize that Brackenridge, or "Brack" for short, would be Tafolla all over again, but on a different level. By third period, someone had set all the trashcans in the boys' bathroom on fire, and it was like a scene from *Mad Max*. A gang unit police car was permanently parked in front of the school. Not a good sign. One of the students wore a parole ankle bracelet because he'd stabbed his father.

At the end of the first month, we had a quiz in biology class. The guy next to me who was friends with ankle bracelet guy asked me if he could copy my test. I was offended and said, "Na, man, we will both get in trouble." He paused for a second, pretending it was all good. Then he punched me so hard that I fell out of my chair—a fate I'd avoided for three years at Tafolla. I got up, then slowly sat back down. I took his paper away from him and decided I would just do his quiz for him.

During the first week of school the entire football team got into a fight with each other in the cafeteria, which I didn't even know was possible. None of it made sense to me.

In math class, one of the football players could smell my nerdiness and all his friends formed a semi-circle around me. I would do the assignment, and then hand it to the left. All of the guys would copy my work, until my assignment made its way back to me. In my nine weeks at Brackenridge, I was already on track with the highest GPA in the whole class to be freshman valedictorian. I had a 100 average in one class and a 110 average in another, something else I didn't even know was possible. The academics felt completely watered down to me.

In the same class, there was an African American guy who was on the football team and always fooling around. I doubt he owned a pencil or pen. One day the teacher, an African American woman, finally got fed up and said, "Jamal, please shut up." He looked at her and fired right back, "Why don't you shut up. How about that?" The class hung in silence for about ten seconds to see what she would do. She retreated and continued with the rest of her lesson even though I was probably the only one paying attention.

CAGE FIGHTS

The locker room at Brack was more terrifying than Tafolla because the guys in it looked more like grown men than students. The changing areas were in super tall cages with doors. If someone closed the door, you'd be locked in a cage in the locker room. The walls of the cages were so high that it always reminded me of the Thunder Dome in *Mad Max*. I always changed as fast as I could to get out of there.

Everyone had PE during the last period of the day, and we could choose the sport we wanted to play. The first part of the period was supposed to be a study hall; we were assigned seats in the cafeteria to study for half an hour before going to PE to play our chosen sport. One day rumor spread that two guys were going to fight in one of those locker room cages.

"Who's going to fight?" I asked the kid "studying" next to me.

"Lester and Big Poppa," the guy replied.

Big Poppa was on the football team and Lester was on the basketball team. Both of these guys were huge and ripped. What made it special though, was that I was assigned to the study hall table where Lester sat. All through study period, I had a front row seat to these two guys staring at each other from across the cafeteria, their eyes pacing back and forth. Sizing each other up and down. I never knew until that moment you could talk trash with your eyes, but these guys were doing it right in front of me. I'm not gonna lie; it was awesome.

At the end of the study period, we were released by sport to go change in the locker room. The football team went first, then the basketball team, and so forth. The locker room was at the complete other end of the campus. The football team was released first, and Big Poppa yelled one last taunt in Lester's direction as he headed to the locker rooms. Our coach was giving the basketball team some ridiculous speech about something. Lester hadn't said a word the entire time and slowly took off all his jewelry while the coach rambled on. He removed his chain, his earring, his rings, everything in preparation for the fight. The coached dismissed the seniors first, and Lester was a senior. The rest of us were dying slow, painful deaths fidgeting, wishing the coach would finish, not wanting to miss the fight.

The coach finally dismissed us, and we ran as fast as our little legs could take us to the cages. By the time we arrived the fight had already started. All we could see were fists swinging. Lester was absolutely dominating Big Poppa. At one point, Lester picked Big Poppa up, turned him upside down, and slammed him down on his head. Big Poppa got up and ran out in complete shame and disgrace.

The basketball team cheered in victory for Lester. We thought we were the toughest guys ever because we were Team Lester. About twenty minutes later, we were all sitting on the basketball court while the coach explained something to us. Then, someone came to the door and said, "Hey, Lester. There's a guy outside that wants to talk to you." Everybody on the basketball team immediately ran away from Lester and left him sitting by himself in the middle of the court—so much for Team Lester.

Big Poppa was outside carrying a gun, and he planned to shoot Lester. The school cop had seen it going down. He snuck up behind Big Poppa, tackled, and arrested him before Lester got shot. I missed the good ol' days when all I had to worry about was a bag of sand in the face.

WHAT THE HELL IS A GAZEBO?

Tafolla had been a time of fear for me. But there was something new at Brackenridge that I was starting to see. I call it, "Things I didn't know were things."

I joined the basketball team at Brackenridge and at our first practice, the coach said we were going to run laps. I was still in the scared Tafolla mode and I anxiously looked around at everyone, trying to figure out how I should behave. The coach said, "All right, we're going to run two miles. You're going to go down this street here. You're going to hit the gazebo, and you're going to come back. Okay, go!"

Everyone took off running and I began to have a panic attack. "WHAT THE HELL IS A GAZEBO?" I thought to myself. I had never ever heard this word before in my entire life. I ran along with everyone else, meanwhile looking frantically around for the gazebo thing we're supposed to run to. I was in a neighborhood I didn't know, so if I missed the gazebo-thing that he was talking about, I'd get lost in this neighborhood, and never get back to school. Something about the sound of it—gazebo—made me think of zoo. Maybe there's something with animals. I continued to run under the hot Texas sun and asked myself, "What the hell is a gazebo?" over and over. I didn't even know how to *spell* gazebo; was it one of those tricky words with silent vowels?

I was freaking out. I looked left and right as I ran and saw that no one else was freaking out, which meant everyone else knew what a gazebo was. How had I missed this? Was there a class where they explained what a gazebo was? I was in absolute panic mode by this point. We ran and ran. I ran as fast as I could to keep up, so I didn't get lost, and so I could see what everyone else saw. The guys at the front reached a decorative little hut thing in the middle of the park. Everybody hit it, then turned around, and began to run back toward our starting point. *This must be it*, I thought. I stopped running, stood there looking at it, and I just got angry.

I didn't have any words for it. How was this thing named "gazebo"? I couldn't have told you what it should have been called. It wasn't a house. It was kind of like a little hut, but it wasn't a hut. It was very nice and decorative. Gazebo.

I was so angry that someone in the world had created this thing that was so obscure that I didn't know about it, and even angrier that it caused me so much anxiety. I remembered from Latin class that the word etymology meant the study of word origins. I wanted someone to study the word gazebo, find out who created it, and go punch them in the face.

SAINT SONIA OF GOMEZ

While I was learning new words like gazebo and helping degenerate classmates cheat on math tests, my sister Sonia was starting her last year at Health Careers. Sonia had done everything she could to help me prepare for my Health Careers application in eighth grade. When I got rejected, she was so concerned for me that she took it upon herself to talk to the principal, Mr. Boyers, at Health Careers one day. Sonia turned on her charm and started her pitch, "Mr. Boyers, you didn't accept my brother, but he's really smart. You should really consider him again. Also, I think he might die if he stays at Brackenridge." Mr. Boyers was so impressed with how bold, articulate, and charming my sister had been that he said, "Tell your brother to come in, and I'll give him an interview."

I went in for an interview. Mom made me bring everything I had to put my case in a positive light: my perfect attendance awards, references from past teachers, and my winning DARE essay. I wanted to show him that I wasn't a bad kid even though I'd failed Latin. I sat there holding my breath—I really wanted out of Brackenridge.

I sat down for my interview with Mr. Boyers. You could tell he was once in the military because every part of his suit was pressed perfectly. He was an impressive man with kind eyes. I thought, "This is what it must have been like to meet George Washington." I don't remember what I told Mr. Boyers that day but I yapped for a while trying to impress him. He didn't say much but quietly read my face, like he was looking into my mind. After about forty-five minutes he told me that he was going to allow me into the school. I was so happy, but I could tell that it had nothing to do with anything I had said and had everything to do with Sonia's influence. My big sister changed my life that day more than she would ever know. In that moment I felt something completely new. It was a mixture of hope and a new beginning. It was the same feeling I got when I listened to the opening instrumental of New Order's song *Ceremony*. Man, it felt good.

Mr. Boyers was one of the nicest guys you ever met. He was the opposite of every administrator I'd met before. Each day, he sat on a bench outside the cafeteria with a big smile on his face, observing his perfect kingdom of Health Careers High School, the school without trouble, fighting, or craziness. It made me happy to see him happy. Each day I thought, "He has the life. He looks like he just won the lottery." It probably made me feel safe too, to see the happy principal outside the cafeteria.

Back at Brackenridge, I took my transfer paper to the Vice Principal. She was angry that the school was losing a "good student." The last person I saw was John, the guy who punched me in biology class. He asked what I was doing, and I told him I was transferring. He got so angry. He said, "What the hell, asshole? Who am I going to copy off of?" I tried not to smirk—not wanting to give him a reason for a parting shot. I shrugged and said, "I don't know, man. Sorry," and walked away giggling and humming *Should I Stay or Should I Go* by The Clash.

HEALTH CAREERS BEGINS

At Brackenridge, students were required to have see-through backpacks and gym bags to make sure no one was carrying a gun. I showed up to Health Careers on my first day with a see-through bag. I was like the French foreign exchange student. No one had ever seen a see-through backpack; apparently guns weren't a problem at Health Careers. I felt a little bit embarrassed and thought to myself, "This is different."

Later that day I had to use the bathroom. I decided that after three long years of holding it in, I was ready to try a public bathroom again. I walked in and immediately ran back out. I was afraid but for a completely different reason. The bathroom as so clean that I thought I had misread the sign and walked into the teachers' bathroom. I was not ready for this level of clean. All of the stalls had toilet paper and doors. There were no puddles of urine on the floor. I stood there in disbelief.

I couldn't wait to tell Danny about my first day at Health Careers. I said, "The craziest thing happened today. These two dudes were walking down the hall and accidentally bumped into each other. They stopped, looked at each other, and then said, 'My bad' and then kept walking. It was crazy. I had never seen anything like it. They bumped into each other. They said they were sorry, and then they went on with their day."

I was so unprepared for a safe environment that it was a total shock to me.

Once I entered Health Careers, I began to understand that the world didn't have to be a place where I was scared all the time. I had only had this feeling one other time, and that is when I would listen to the song *Story of My Life* by Social Distortion. It was the feeling that maybe there were some stories that had happy endings. After the first day and the weeks that followed, I thought it would be pretty good—and it was.

TROJAN WARS

I transferred mid-semester from Brackenridge to Health Careers and I went from being on track to Valedictorian to risking having to repeat the grade. My English teacher, Ms. Fishbeck, had to give me incomplete grades for the first semester because I hadn't read the books my classmates had already read. She could have failed me, but the incomplete grades softened the blow, which was encouraging as I started my new academic pursuits.

I stayed after school a couple times to get caught up with her, and in talking she learned I worked at the HEB supermarket. That particular HEB was in a bad neighborhood that bordered on the wealthier historic neighborhood of San Antonio called Monticello Park. Ms. Fishbeck lived in

Monticello Park, and when she found out I walked home from that HEB, she was concerned. She wrote her phone number on a piece of paper and said, "You're not allowed to walk home in that neighborhood. If you do, you call me, and I will drop you off at home." I never called her, but I remember thinking it was the sweetest thing that any teacher had ever done for me. It also demonstrated the care and interest the teachers had for the students at Health Careers.

My geography teacher, Ms. Muenster, was a legend and was the first person to ever plant the seed in me to travel the world. Her class wasn't just about maps and political borders but about the culture and people of different places. We remained in touch, and years later, I had to confess that I cheated on one test in her class. It took a lot to admit that to her, but I couldn't have that hanging between us if I was going to maintain an adult friendship with her.

The teacher who had the greatest impact, ironically, was my Latin teacher, Mr. Lehmann. His class was so outrageously hard, but he'd do anything and everything to help you answer a question and learn. He'd get angry if another classmate whispered the answer to you while he was trying to act out the answer so you would at least learn something. He was an amazing teacher and one of the top three storytellers I've heard in my life. He would stand on his desk to act out the stories told in Latin literature. One semester he was telling the story of the Trojan War. I knew we'd be tested on it later and was frantically taking notes. I was getting more and more frustrated as he told the story because I realized I couldn't take awesome notes and take in all the story. Mr. Lehmann was such a good storyteller that it was like watching a movie! Finally, I gave up and made a decision to stop notetaking and simply listen. It was such a good story, I wanted to take it all in. I put my pen down and made a conscious decision to fail the test—turns out I learned better through listening to stories and passed the test anyway.

After hearing his story of the Trojan War, I bought the book *Mythology* by Edith Hamilton, *The Iliad,* and *The Odyssey* by Homer, which were the texts he taught from. I wanted more of that style of storytelling. Little by little, during that awesome time at Health Careers, I was shedding the baggage I had from Tafolla.

SMART KIDS AND BAGELS

Because you had to apply, the entire student population was motivated to be at Health Careers. Kids didn't cause trouble because, one, they weren't troublemakers, and two, if they did cause trouble, they'd get kicked back to their home school. Health Careers had an entire population of students whose parents cared about what their kids were doing and how they were behaving. The students there had ambition like I'd never seen, and Health Careers gave them an opportunity to use it.

At Tafolla, being smart was a bad brand so you sort of had to hide it. At Health Careers, it was the complete opposite. I'd see kids reading novels while they were waiting for class to begin, and I even saw two guys spend their lunchtime in the library researching facts for a debate they were having during another class. Who does that?

Wei-Han Tan was the smartest guy in my whole class. He posted a flyer that he was starting a bio-engineering club. I had no idea what that meant, but thought it sounded hella smart. I understood the kind of people who were at the school. I thought it was awesome that this dude was starting a bio-engineering club.

I wasn't as smart as that, and I was often reminded of how much I didn't know.

My sister Sonia was a senior when I was a freshman at Health Careers. She came home one day and told me that she got a job at this place called Big Apple Bagel. I sat there in silence, trying to process what she was telling me.

"What the hell is a bagel?"

She described it to me. I was sixteen and confused. I said, "Let me get this straight. You are describing a donut, but it's not a donut. It's round like a donut. It looks like a donut. You can put sweet stuff like cream cheese on it to make it sweet like a donut. Why wouldn't they just make it a donut?" She got more frustrated as she tried to explain that you could also make the bagel into a sandwich. In return, I told her it was nonsense. I accused her of wanting to be white and go to college because she was having bagels.

A few days later she brought me a bagel sandwich. I got even angrier. Not only had she confused the whole donut idea, now she was complicating the sandwich process. "Why can't you just make a sandwich on normal bread?"

I was overwhelmed by the same angry, frustrated, why-didn't-someone-tell-me feeling I'd had when I learned the word gazebo. I was frustrated because I felt stupid, and I didn't want to feel stupid. Someone should have told me there were things out there called bagels before. Why did I have to wait until I was sixteen years old to find out what a bagel was?

FRIENDS FOR LIFE

Brackenridge was a school of about twenty-five hundred kids, whereas my graduating class at Health Careers had no more than two hundred. I felt like I knew everyone.

Not long after I transferred to Health Careers, I started to make friends. I was sitting by myself one day. A group of outgoing students was talking nearby. One of the guys from the group came over to me and said, "Hey, you should hang out with us." Up to that point in my life, it was the craziest thing I've ever experienced. I'd never been invited to join a group that was already formed. I didn't know any of them and they were inviting me to hang out with them. That blew my mind.

My default reaction was, "Hey, man, thanks a lot. I appreciate it, but I'm good. Thank you." I was overwhelmed with the thought of meeting that many new people at once. Some of my fear and anxiety surfaced about this new thing—joining a group—that I didn't know how to do. It felt so good that someone had asked me, though. By asking, he told me, "We think you're worth hanging out with or being around." Health Careers brought about so many new feelings for me: safety, acceptance, invitation. I felt great.

I was riding the bus from Health Careers to the hospital where we interned one morning and heard someone in front of me debating another person. I turned around and listened, thinking, "This dude is smart. Really smart. I need to make him my friend." I'd never so intentionally wanted to be someone's friend, but somehow, I knew being friends with this intelligent guy would be a good thing for me. His name was Dax Moreno. Not only was he way smarter than me but he also had a super cool name. Life just isn't fair sometimes.

Then one day I met a guy in Latin class named Luke, who ended up becoming one of my other lifelong friends. Luke, Dax, and I were in yearbook at Health Careers two years in a row. Luke was the computer guy and taught me about the internet. He was the first guy I ever met that was knee-deep in this thing called the internet. Unbeknownst to all of us, he was running a side business during yearbook class and one year he made over fifteen thousand dollars. I can't tell you what it was, to protect the innocent, but let's just say it involved music and the internet.

Luke and I also bonded over music. When I told him my favorite Weezer song was *My Name is Jonas,* he proceeded to tell me everything he knew about them. When I told him my favorite Everclear song was *Santa Monica*, he told me about a band the lead singer was in before Everclear, called Colorfinger, and it blew my mind.

Without Luke and Dax, I would never have gotten into technology. Luke was a nice, cool, intelligent guy. He came from a big family like mine. My parents were okay with my music obsession, and Luke's parents were okay with his computer obsession.

Luke was the first person I knew who explored the world in an overt yet safe way. If there was a mysterious door somewhere, he'd walk over to open it, curious to know what was inside. My Tafolla brain said, "Don't go in there. Bad things can hurt you." Luke was just exploring the world, and if someone said, "Hey, don't go in there," he was cool with it and simply closed the door.

I shed part of my trauma during Health Careers. I started eating lunch again as a senior in Health Careers because of Luke and Dax. Dax had a used Hyundai that he was very proud of. We'd go to the gas station during our lunch period and buy a slushy and a hot dog for three or four dollars. It was awesome to leave the school campus in the middle of the day and not worry about getting shot. Few things felt better than the freedom of driving around with Dax and listening to *Santeria* by Sublime.

AND THEN THERE WAS A GIRL

Rachelle walked in to study hall as the room began to fill. I got there early so I could claim a chair in the very back, which was my routine because it's where I felt safe—I hadn't shed all my habits from Tafolla. She, on the other hand, headed straight for the front row and announced to no one in particular, "I'm going to sit in the front because I want to be the center of attention." I had two immediate conflicting thoughts: "I hate everything about that girl. Who sits in the front row in study hall?" and "Man, she's pretty." I'd never seen anyone with straighter hair than Rachelle. "How does she get her hair so straight?" I wondered. "Is it natural? Maybe it is a white person thing. Who knows." But the worst thing of all was how endearing I found her brashness.

A few periods later, I had another class on medical terminology with her. I thought, "Oh, there's that girl I can't stand," and went to sit on the other side of the room. No sooner had I sat down than the teacher told us that she preferred to have us in assigned seats—in high school! She moved me to the desk directly behind Rachelle, who turned around and said with the biggest smile, "Hi! I'm Rachelle." This was the very first time in my entire life that a beautiful girl had gone out of her way to talk to me, and it made me feel funny. My inner punk rocker was screaming, "Don't you dare like her, asshole. Don't do it. Sure she smells amazing, has a great sense of humor, and is super intelligent, but remember that annoying thing she said? You need to hate her."

I couldn't help myself. I really tried, but she was just too charming. Her smile was a tractor beam and her taste in music was on a level with my brother Danny, which I didn't think was possible. We played this game where I tried to avoid talking to her, and she would look at me, blink, and I would fold like a cheap lawn chair. I didn't know what flirting was. I had to admit she was kind of cool, even though I was trying not to like her.

When we started studying the Roman Empire in Latin class, Mr. Lehmann explained that he had a tradition called Toga Day. To my horror all the students were supposed to wear a toga to school and if you didn't, you'd get a zero for that portion of the Latin assignment. The rules were that you had to wear the toga even if you didn't have Latin class on Toga Day, and Mr. Lehmann would visit the other classrooms to make sure you were wearing your toga. I hated it. I risked the zero because there was no way I was trading my flannel shirt and Nirvana T-shirt for a toga. I was quiet, and I thought I could hide from him. I didn't have Latin that day, but Mr. Lehmann walked into the medical terminology class. He looked around and turned to leave. I had pulled it off! He absolutely missed me, and I was almost scott-free, until Rachelle called out to him as he was leaving and said, "Mr. Lehmann, Lorenzo's not wearing his toga!" I wanted to kill her as she gave me the flirtiest giggle-smirk in Health Careers history. I had never felt this before. I hated her, and I liked her at the same time. The old Lorenzo would have demanded revenge and hellfire to rain down. The new Lorenzo wanted to make her a mix tape, punch her in the arm, and run my hands through that *pinche* straight hair. Why was it so straight!? Anyway, it cost me a zero that day.

The silent flirtation and talking went on, but I didn't have a clue how to move my like-hate relationship with Rachelle in any direction. The next semester, I was having trouble with anatomy class. The anatomy teacher, Mrs. Knight, had a soft spot for me and asked if I wanted to help her grade papers during my study hall period. I was thrilled, because study hall was boring, and I didn't use it to study anyway. Mrs. Knight kept a ball python named Willoughby, and she'd let me feed mice to Willoughby. I thought that was so cool.

I was loving life. I had about three weeks of peace and quiet. I stopped going to study hall, because I had a pass to go to Mrs. Knight's lab. Then one day I walked into Mrs. Knight's class to grade papers, but Mrs. Knight wasn't there. Instead, Rachelle was sitting on the lab stool wearing a shit-eating grin. She had found out where I was and got a pass to grade papers with me.

My punk rocker side was outraged that I was so excited Rachelle had found me and gone out of her way to be where I was. I gave up trying to hate her and sat down. The rest I couldn't explain even if I tried. It was like listening to my favorite New Order song, *Temptation*, every single day I was with her. And just like the song, it made my heart pound with feelings that young men try to explain for the rest of their lives.

OPPORTUNITY AND AFFIRMATION

DEAR LENCH,

An important question needs to be pondered: What are you going to do with the opportunities life presents to you? Are you going to piss them away or are you going to wrestle them to the ground?

Health Careers was the first time you were given amazing opportunities to befriend people who would change your life. You had the chance to learn from people who were amazing. To your credit, you took advantage of all of it and I am so proud of you for that. Keep doing that.

You need to look for your seasons of opportunity. What will you do when the Universe finally serves up something good? Will you run away from it because you're afraid that you don't know what to do with it? Or, will you embrace it and take it for all it's worth? Danny always used to say that you have life by the balls. This is what he was talking about.

Your life didn't become perfect at Health Careers, but you were no longer afraid of anyone hurting you. You didn't have to be afraid of the bathroom, locker room, or cafeteria. You realized that many people in the world are kind.

Health Careers was the first place where you felt the

safety that you should have been feeling a long time ago. And with safety in place, you took up the grand adventure of exploration. Sure you started exploring the world a little later, and that's a great thing—better late than never.

I want you to know, too, that your past, your present, and your future are three completely separate things. Yes, you went to Tafolla and had a horrible experience, but that experience is in the past. The decisions you make today are the only ones that matter.

In the past, exploring the world was dangerous and could have hurt you. You saw it hurt the people that you loved and cared about.

At Health Careers you decided to start exploring, and that's the way healthy people work and operate. The awesome thing, Lench, is that you did it. It was your decision. No one can make you do it, and no one can decide for you. Only you can decide for yourself.

CHARGE ON, MIGHTY *TORO*

As we come to the end of our grand tale, I want to do something for you that has been on my heart for a long time. I want to speak a word of encouragement to you that I wish someone had spoken to me so many years ago.

Lencho, I know you and I know what you have been through. I know that in the past you have not felt like the brave bull that Hemingway wrote about. I know that in the past you have done and said things that you wish you could take back.

Know that all of that is in the past and none of it matters now. What matters now is that you hear the words I am about to speak into your life.

You are Lorenzo Gomez III. You are a one in a million Tafolla *Toro*. You are the *Toro* that was forged in the fires of heaven and there is no one else like you. You are the most special *Toro* I have ever known or ever will know.

You are wild and dangerous and a marvel to behold. You are the *Toro* that will find his own way in the world. The good book says that you were created a little lower than the angels in heaven.

You are the *Toro* that will climb mountains and travel this world. You are the *Toro* that will be stabbed in the heart by life and live to charge it again. You are the *Toro* that will love, laugh, and will forge unbreakable friendships.

You are the *Toro* with adventure in his heart and eternity in his soul.

You are that kind of *Toro*. Only the wise *toro* knows that he cannot change the past. And only the foolish *toro* worries about tomorrow. But dare to charge just today and it will make you the bravest *toro* of them all,

Ole.

CONCLUSION

A MENTAL HEALTH JOURNEY

It's 2019. I'm 38 years old. I'm listening to Grey Cell Green *by Ned's Atomic Dustbin.*

I carry around a pen with me at all times that I had engraved with the numbers 3-3-16. Those numbers stand for March 3, 2016, which was the day my therapist Marney walked me through all of the fear and anxiety that I wrote about in this book. He introduced mental health into my life and gave me tools that helped me put the fear and anxiety in its proper place.

During one of our sessions, he asked me to write a letter to my parents telling them a lot of what I wrote about in this book. Part of that letter was telling them I knew they did their best and appreciated it, but here and now, I am the adult and I can take care of me going forward. It may sound ridiculous and cliché, but March 3, 2016, was the first time I felt like I was an adult.

Starting my mental health journey has been one of the most transformational decisions of my adult life. And because of that I want to close this book with four thoughts I think can help you start your journey.

EVERYONE NEEDS RECOVERY

My pastor Doug has said for years that everyone is in need of recovery to some degree or another. He is absolutely right. No one escapes childhood without a little baggage and that is okay. No one is perfect, your parents especially—no offense to your parents. All of us along the way pick up one bad habit or another as kids. And just like seeds planted in the ground, they will grow into full-blown dysfunction if you are not actively working on them.

It doesn't mean you are broken or damaged. It just means you are a card-carrying member of the human race, like the rest of us.

MENTAL HEALTH IS NOT MENTAL ILLNESS

The term Mental Health has been incorrectly branded to a lot of people. To some, it means mental illness. Or that you are just plain crazy. This could not be further from the truth. I have a family member that is a diagnosed paranoid schizophrenic. They literally hear voices in their head and have to take prescription medicine to deal with them. That is mental illness.

Mental health is about having the tools and strategies to successfully deal with your emotions, thoughts, and decisions. One is a medical condition that you have no control over. The other is healthy actions and habits you choose to engage in, like working out.

MENTAL HEALTH AFFECTS EVERYTHING ELSE

The internet is full of gym selfies and fit bodies. I'd like to start a trend of posting mental health selfies and fit minds. Why? Because mental health is the first step before anything else. It affects every other aspect of your life.

You can have washboard abs, a low-carb diet, and the best job in the world, but none of it will matter if your mind is not renewed daily. Your mental health has the power to make all those aspects better or undo all the work you have done in those areas. And it all starts in the mind.

FIND A COACH OR COUNSELOR

And just like having a trainer at the gym, you probably need a mental health coach to get you on the right track. I see a therapist that has been doing this work for decades and has a personality that I gel with. He is wise and patient, but also no-nonsense when it comes to these principles. He knows that the stakes are high and is a true professional.

And just like a good trainer, he knows that part of his job is to give me tools and exercises that I can use when he is not around. Tools that I can practice every day when my mental health goes up and down. This is what you need to find, and when you do, you will start living the life you are supposed to live.

This list is not exhaustive and doesn't have all the answers. It's not supposed to. It's supposed to point you in the right direction, just like someone did for me. And I am proud to say that if you got to the end of this book, you have already received two double barrels of mental health principles. So the good news is that you have already started your mental health journey.

I hope you decide to keep going and remember, today is all that matters.

ACKNOWLEDGMENTS

There are so many people to thank in their support of me during the writing of this book. I want to thank my family for their unbelievable support and encouragement. Mom, Pops, Danny, Tara, Denise, Marco, Martha, Hector, Sonia, Jeff, Mari, Roland, and Patty. Thank you to my nieces and nephews Andrea, Richard, Devina, Brandon, Markie, Joshua, Noah, Elisha, David, and Oliva. Without you I would not be who I am, and each day that passes, I love you more.

Thank you to all my friends and personal board members who are constantly there to guide me, give me counsel and feedback. Dax Moreno, Luke Owen, Emily Bowe, Randy Smith, Khaled Saffouri, Pravesh Mistry, Bill Schley, Jake and DJ Gracia, Steve and Marisa Cunningham.

Thank you, Alex Blanchard, for letting me think through many of these concepts while trying to avoid leg day.

I want to say thank you to my teammates and colleagues for being so patient with me while I finished this book. Alexandra Frey, David Garcia, Charles Woodin, Jon Garcia, Laurie Leiker—I could not have finished without your support and help.

Thank you to Mario Guajardo and all the entrepreneurs at Broadway News. You continually were a source for inspiration and creativity when I was struggling.

Thank you to all the Geekdom Media family of thought partners and collaborators. Alex Hilmy, Jaime Cooke, John Largent, Michael Largent, Jason Barrera, Kathy Kersten, Carlos Maestas, Jennifer Maestas, Cara Nichols, Kerry Litzenberg, Codie Wright, and Rob La Gesse.

Thank you to my City Church small group. I will never forget the prayers you have said for me and this book. Thank you Jess, Tim, Cody, Aly, Stormie, Lauren, Thomas, and Onnalea.

Thank you to all the Tafolla *Toros* both past and present. Thank you to Diego Bernal, Stephanie Guerra, Michelle Martinez, and Jose De La Cruz who still rock *Toro* Power to this day.

Thank you to the Burnt Nopal team for making yet another amazing cover that I am absolutely in love with. Cruz Ortiz, Olivia Ortiz, and Lenzy Mora, thank you so much.

Thank you to the Scribe team for helping me bring this book into the world. Specifically, thank you to Barbara Boyd. You are a lighthouse to me, and your encouragement, guidance, and counsel I will never fully be able to thank you for. Thank you also to Kayla Sokol and Greg Larson for your help and support. Thank you to JT, Zach, and Tucker. You have created something truly special.

Thank you to Ed Rister, Cara Collins, Merritt Weeks, Katie Chain, Jeanne Russell, Jana Kennelly, and Marjie French for being so encouraging to my writing.

Last, but not least, thank you to Graham Weston, Doug Robins, and Marney DeFoore. The world of mental health has become so dear to me and it is because of you. Thank you for this gift.

ABOUT THE AUTHOR

It's very important for you to know that I am wearing a Pearl Jam shirt in this picture.

LORENZO GOMEZ III grew up in a Hispanic neighborhood in inner-city San Antonio. In the early 1990s, Lorenzo's neighborhood had the highest percentage of drive-by shootings and gang violence in all of San Antonio. He spent three years of middle school living in fear of being ridiculed, beat up, or worse—and lived to tell his tale.

Today, Lorenzo is an expert in ecosystem development, a CEO, a public speaker, an author, and a podcast host. He has successfully helped convert a dormant urban sector of San Antonio into a thriving entrepreneurial hub. Over the last ten years, he has effectively engaged others in his vision and orchestrated their skills and strengths to create a new contemporary community of technology companies.

Under Lorenzo's direction, Geekdom became one of the top twenty-five coworking sites in the world (2016). Geekdom has grown from its humble beginnings as a small coworking space, to its current membership of over 1,900 entrepreneurs, businesses, and freelancers from around San Antonio.

In 2011, Lorenzo was tapped by Graham Weston, co-founder of Rackspace, to be Executive Director of The 80/20 Foundation, a philanthropic organization that works with and funds new and emerging nonprofits whose focus is on building the San Antonio technology ecosystem. In the last seven years, The 80/20 Foundation has given grants to nonprofit programs such as Venture for America, Students Plus Startups, and The Open Cloud Institute.

As the current Chairman of the Board for both Geekdom and The 80/20 Foundation, Lorenzo has had a positive impact on the tech industry in San Antonio, the city's economic growth, and revitalization of the area. Within the five-year development period, Geekdom, at the heart of the downtown tech district, has experienced a 1,000 percent membership growth, and those members have generated over a hundred new jobs and $95 million in capital.

Mr. Gomez, a compelling storyteller, is the author of *The Cilantro Diaries: Business Lessons from the Most Unlikely Places*, the story of how he went from the stockroom of a grocery store to the boardrooms of two private companies, without a college degree. In his inspiring and humorous style, readers have found a story of hope and accomplishment, dedication and success. In the first week of publication, *The Cilantro Diaries* was ranked #1 in four separate categories on Amazon, including Vocational Guidance, Careers, Schools & Teaching, and Career Development. The audiobook was the #1 New Release the week it debuted on audible.com, and it continues to be a top pick in the business categories, for both print and audio.

In March 2018, Mr. Gomez teamed with nationally-recognized branding expert, Bill Schley, to create The Brand Brothers podcast, focusing on branding and marketing. Between them, Gomez and Schley bring their own unique perspectives on business marketing—both good and not so good—along with great conversation and fun. Within the first week of launch, The Brand Brothers hit the overall top 100 and #9 business podcast on iTunes.

Geekdom Media is Lorenzo's newest startup venture. He co-founded Geekdom Media with serial entrepreneur, Graham Weston, with the mission to bring original content to the San Antonio ecosystem. Inspired by the impact and success of his first book, Lorenzo is now tapping other San Antonio thought leaders to bring their skills and experience to the masses. Geekdom Media will be helping them produce high-quality, relevant books and podcasts, to introduce these thought leaders to a broader audience.

Made in the USA
Columbia, SC
30 June 2021